私房菜

DUMPLiNG
DAUGHTER

COVER PHOTO BY **Ellysia Francovitch**.
COVER AND BOOK DESIGN BY **Holly Gordon Perez**.

私房菜

DUMPLiNG DAUGHTER

HEIRLOOM RECIPES

from our RESTAURANTS AND HOME KITCHENS

NADIA LIU SPELLMAN

RECIPES BY **SALLY LING**

CONTENTS

RECIPE LIST

HOW IT ALL BEGAN...

No one can choose their parents, but I hit the jackpot with mine. My dad was an outstanding communicator, filled with knowledge and rich experiences to share, a true renaissance man. My mom has always led by example. Smart, beautiful, and quick-witted, she is one of the strongest women I know.

Their lives began in China, sixteen years apart, between World War II and the establishment of the People's Republic of China. After two very different journeys, they came together with a shared passion for food, dining, and hospitality. Their first venture together, Sally Ling's, is one of their biggest accomplishments—although I'm sure they'd both say it was their kids. I had the privilege of growing up with Sally Ling's, where I experienced the finest luxuries in food and service from the inside. I learned everything I know about food and entertaining from my parents. As I grow older, I realize more and more how their lives have directly shaped who I am. I consider myself incredibly lucky to have spent so much time learning from both of them throughout the different stages of my life.

And because of that, it is my honor to share their stories in this book. I've always been so proud to say my parents created Sally Ling's, and love to tell the story of how it all began... with my dad's craving for Chinese food that led him right to my mom's restaurant in Chinatown. The rest, as they say, is history—but we need to back up a ways to get there.

IN 1949, when the Communist party took control of China, the Nationalists retreated to Taiwan alongside their leader Chiang Kai-shek. My grandfather, Lau Yie, was a navigation pilot with the Chinese Air Force and moved his family to Taiwan along with over two million Nationalist refugees. My grandmother, Lau Lau, grew up in a prominent family in Beijing and insisted that they bring a nanny with them to Taiwan. My mom, Sally Ling, was born and raised in Taiwan until she was fourteen years old. Over the years, Lau Yie grew tired of the air force. He often feared for his life—once he got on the plane, there was no guarantee he'd make it home alive. He cared deeply for his family and didn't want to leave them prematurely, so he retired in 1963.

It was difficult to find a job in Taiwan as a retired pilot. Lau Lau's father was a University of Illinois alum from the 1920s and always glorified the United States. Lau Yie's best friend had recently emigrated to Brazil, which was seen as a steppingstone to America, so they followed his best friend to Sao Paolo. (This time without the nanny.)

When they arrived in Brazil, Lau Lau and Lau Yie opened a gift shop, which they ran and operated together. Sally was fourteen and had never cooked before, but she learned so the family could eat dinner together each night. She grew to love shopping at the street market to find ingredients for dinner.

With no experience in the kitchen, Sally tried her best to remember all the dishes her nanny made. She experimented with dough, using yeast to make buns, and rolling out dumpling skins. Lau Lau's favorite foods were dumplings and noodles, and Sally and her sister Wilma wanted to please her by recreating the dishes from their life in Taiwan. Lau Yie loved seafood, so they bought fresh jumbo shrimp. There were very few Chinese restaurants in Brazil, so the family relied on Sally for the

nostalgic tastes of home. Their compliments encouraged her to keep cooking and trying new dishes. She began to perfect breads, pancakes, and noodles, which brought her deep satisfaction.

For a time, America remained a faraway, foreign land; nothing more than a dream. But it remained the goal: my mom learned English so she could one day study in America. The principal of her high school recommended a few colleges to apply to in America. Because of their tight finances, they choose the school with the lowest tuition. In 1968, Sally joined Wilma at the University of Missouri in Rolla, where she studied applied mathematics and computer science. Her time there wasn't easy. The language barrier made it very difficult, and she had to study that much harder than her classmates. She quickly realized she did not like the food in the dorm. But there were some good moments that year, like celebrating her first American holiday—Thanksgiving, which she and Wilma spent at a professor's home. She was intrigued by the concept of an American Thanksgiving and grew to love the holiday.

When the dorms closed for winter vacation that first year, she and Wilma traveled to stay with their uncle and aunt in Texas. Sally was so grateful that she had a place to stay over break that she offered to cook dinner for their family of five. They loved her cooking and said they'd never tasted such good Chinese food. Naturally, she ended up cooking dinner each night until she returned to school.

Back at school in rural Missouri, money was hard to come by. Sally was turned down from a $1/hour babysitting job for a five-year-old girl because her English wasn't strong enough. During her junior year, she had $60 in her bank account. She soon learned how to eat for a dollar a day—she bought ground pork, scallions, and Pillsbury biscuits on sale for ten cents a can. She then wrapped the pork and scallions in the biscuit dough and steamed them. Just like that, she had delicious pork buns to keep her full all day long. I heard this story a lot growing up, as my mom always reminded me of how lucky my sisters and I were.

After graduating in 1972, Sally quickly married. Her first husband was a successful restauranteur and she moved with him to New York City, where she was a stay-at-home mom to my older sister, Christina. Staying at home did not suit Sally. She applied for a job on Wall

Street and was offered an annual salary of $50,000. Her husband didn't believe a wife should work, so he made her a deal: he'd pay her the same amount (weekly, in cash) to not work and stay home. My mother took his money, saved every penny, and every two weeks deposited it to her savings account. Ultimately this lifestyle was unfulfilling, and her marriage ended in divorce.

Then came the moment that changed everything. My mom's aunt came to visit from Boston and remarked that there wasn't a single acceptable Chinese restaurant in that city. Lau Yie, who had worked in restaurants before, heard this and thought it might be a big opportunity. He suggested that the family move to Boston to open a restaurant. At first, Sally thought he was crazy, but coming from a Buddhist background, she firmly believed in filial piety. She always did everything she could to make her parents happy and felt the burden to support them as they grew older. Suddenly, this crazy idea became a real chance to help her parents make a living.

Sally took a trip to Boston to hunt for a strong restaurant location. She found a space in Beacon Hill, and with the money she'd saved, set out to open her first restaurant. In just two weeks, she completed a $250,000 build out (with the help of her architect uncle, Paul Sun), hired a top chef, and opened The Great Wall. The Great Wall was a massive success from its opening, receiving great acclaim and a 3-star review from *The Boston Globe*.

Sally launched the restaurant, but it was Lau Yie and Lau Lau who ran it day to day. At that time, my mom worked as a computer programmer to make a living for herself and my sister Christina, who was only five years old at the time. Any money the restaurant made went to her parents. Unfortunately, despite the great press, the location lacked parking, and after two years, The Great Wall closed its doors. (I remember showing my mom a potential location for Dumpling Daughter. We drove around for ten minutes looking for parking. Before we even stepped foot in the space, she told me it wasn't going to work. Her first restaurant failed because of parking, and she wasn't going to let me make the same mistake.) Sally, while discouraged, learned a very expensive lesson and was determined to make back her money. Today, she jokes that she spent $250,000 to find her father a job.

After The Great Wall closed, a chef from Joyce Chen's restaurant asked my mom to partner with him in opening a restaurant. She naively agreed, and a short three months later, he promptly bought her out of her portion. Later, she realized her partner was only using her for her knowledge and connections to the bank. Another lesson learned, but at least this time, it didn't cost quite as much.

One afternoon, on a routine visit to Chinatown's Shawmut Bank, Sally learned of a restaurant space available for $500 a month at 10 Tyler Street: a walk-up located across the street from Chinatown's only parking lot. She took her life lessons and gave the restaurant business another shot. This time, parking was plentiful!

Peking Cuisine opened in 1979 and was an instant success. Peking Cuisine was a family-run business through and through: Lau Yie mixed strong Polynesian drinks, Lau Lau helped with front of the house operations, and my uncle was a waiter. Lau Lau worked lunch and Lau Yie worked dinner late into the night—they loved every minute. Lau Yie spent his afternoons sitting at the bar talking to customers and employees. Late at night, he entertained the many college students who frequented the establishment. (My mom attributes a large part of Peking Cuisine's success to the fact that they were one of three restaurants in Chinatown with a liquor license and could stay open until 2 AM.) Sally was thrilled: This was her first restaurant that featured her own homestyle cooking. And this time she'd succeeded in finding her parents jobs.

Peking Cuisine was packed on weekends, and it was the go-to, late-night spot for college students. Their beef noodle soup, pan-seared pork buns, and pork and napa cabbage dumplings were the talk of the town. (All staples at Dumpling Daughter today. Good food is timeless!) Peking Cuisine not only proved my mom to be a successful entrepreneur, but it was also how she met my father. The third restaurant was the charm.

MY FATHER, EDWARD NAN LIU, was a scholar and a businessman from New York City. One of his many passions was driving nice cars, so he started Budget Rent-A-Car of Metropolitan New York, which allowed him to drive exotic cars as a company investment. One weekend, he and his good friend visited Boston. Craving Chinese food, they headed to Chinatown, the only place to find Chinese food in Boston at that time. He and his friend walked the neighborhood, finding only Cantonese restaurants, until they stumbled upon Peking Cuisine. Based on the name, he thought it was safe to assume it would feature a Mandarin-speaking staff. They were the first table of the day and promptly ordered kung pao chicken, buns, noodles, spring rolls, and lobster with ginger and scallion. (Sally was working in the kitchen that day and thought to herself: Who the hell is eating lobster for lunch??) When they were still dining two-and-a-half hours later, my mom came out of the kitchen, upset that the table couldn't be turned. She asked if they were enjoying their meal. Edward, smoking a pipe, gallantly said, "Well, do you want to know the truth or something that sounds good?" Sally answered energetically, "The truth, of course!" He proceeded to critique each dish, telling her, "I think your food is good for Boston, homestyle and clean, but it's not close to what we have in New York."

> "The epic lunch finally ended with Edward's friend saying, "Liu Nan, give her your card and invite her to New York for Chinese food. If you don't, I will.""

Sally could tell he was a connoisseur, unlike the customers she typically met in her dining room. When asked if her parents owned the restaurant, she proudly answered that she was, in fact, the owner. The epic lunch finally ended with Edward's friend saying, "Liu Nan, give her your card and invite her to New York for Chinese food. If you don't, I will." Over the years, my father told this story again and again, always describing my mom as beautiful and capable but having a lot to learn about Chinese food. He thought it was unlikely that she would call, but when she did within a few short weeks—from a payphone in the Upper East Side, no less!—he was pleasantly surprised and admired her tenacity. (He canceled his date with a local girl that night to take out his surprise out-of-town guest.)

The first restaurant he took her to was not the most extravagant, but she was impressed by the authenticity of the menu, which reminded her of her childhood in Taiwan. Next, he took her to Mr. K's, the most expensive and upscale Chinese restaurant in Manhattan during its time. Looking back, this was typical of my dad. He liked taking us to the best places—but also the modest places serving great food, so that we could appreciate both luxury and authenticity. Mr. K's made the biggest impression on my mom. That restaurant experience was life changing. White tablecloths, fine art, exquisite cuisine, and impeccable service—there was nothing like that in Boston.

Now it was Sally's turn to invite Edward back to Boston. There was no doubt she wanted to impress him but knew no restaurant in Boston could compare to what she'd experienced in New York. Coincidentally, she had many friends who went to National Taiwan University, the same school as Edward, so she decided to invite them all over for a grand meal—this was her chance to impress him. Unlike the homestyle fare at Peking Cuisine, she planned an elaborate twelve-course banquet for twelve people, including elegant and rare dishes comprised of sea cucumber, abalone, whole fish, and lobster. My dad later admitted that he thought there was no way a young, single mom would be a passable cook, and ate before arriving. After dinner, he professed his stupidity—the food was nothing short of fantastic! This was the first time my mom realized that her cooking came from a place of love. My dad used to say his two favorite chefs were his older sister and my mom, because they cooked with pure love and femininity. He said my mom's food was fine, light, and clean.

Edward enjoyed the bachelor life in Manhattan (including dating a few movie stars and a former Miss Universe), but he was hard to impress and never felt the need to settle down—until he met Sally. At the same time, Sally was enthralled by Edward. She admired him for his seemingly endless knowledge—his fluency in both Chinese and English and his expertise in multiple subjects of history were amongst his most admirable qualities. History was always my mom's weakest subject, and she loved learning from him. She knew she wanted to win his heart, and she knew how: through her food.

Sally's desire to entertain and open an upscale restaurant in Boston only continued to grow. After five years, Peking Cuisine could no longer offer what she wanted to provide—a formal dining room, tableside service, and fine Chinese cuisine. When a two-story restaurant became available on Commercial Street in the North End, she was immediately interested. It had a steep asking price of $1.4 million, but the second floor of the building featured a room large enough to host banquets for 120 people. She would be in good company, too: next door was the famed restaurant Jasper, owned by renowned Boston chef Jasper White. This location, the success of Peking Cuisine, and having my dad as a business partner made it possible to make her dream come true.

In 1981, Sally and Edward married, and they began to build their dream restaurant together. Inspiration for the design and décor was drawn straight from Mr. K's. They honeymooned in Hong Kong to find the finest china, silver, and art. Intricate gold carvings lined the walls in custom built shelves (the same ones we display at Dumpling Daughter). To replicate the china from the palace in Hong Kong, they ordered custom plates to be hand-painted with the restaurant's logo, two phoenixes intertwined.

In addition to the décor, there was a particular emphasis placed on the importance of fine service.

A visit to Sally Ling's promised freshly pressed white linens, French-style cart service with tableside plating, and tuxedoed waiters. Sally hired her aunt, an award-winning floral designer in Taiwan, to create fresh flower arrangements. Customers would return week after week if only to see the sleek modern arrangements.

The menu was elegant, with fewer than twenty dishes, in addition to three prix fixe dinner options. In 1985, one of the most popular dishes, Lobster with Fresh Ginger and Scallions, appeared on the front cover of Boston Magazine as the most expensive dish in Boston. (It went for $79.95.) The wine list featured over five hundred bottles of wine, and you couldn't go without Louis XIII Cognac for an after-dinner drink. Their head chef came from a top restaurant in New York, and despite his experience and pedigree, my mom always worked with him to create new menu items to introduce her ideas.

In 1986, my parents invited a delegation of Boston-area chefs, including CK Sau, Sally Ling's executive chef, Jasper White of Jasper, and Moncef Meddeb of L'Espalier, on a life-changing trip to China. My father planned the itinerary for the two-week trip, making arrangements to be hosted by the Chinese government at each stop. The goal was cultural exchange through food—China was in the midst of opening to the West, after years of turmoil wrought by the Cultural Revolution.

During those hard years, creativity and intellectualism were attacked to bring more control to the Communist government, and traditional Chinese cooking suffered huge setbacks. There were virtually no chefs trained in China for decades, until finally older chefs in their 70s were brought in to teach a new, younger generation in their 20s. The absence of the older generation's expertise also meant that the knowledge of how to cook for Western guests was lost. This trip was part of an effort to invite American chefs into professional Chinese kitchens to elevate the status of China's fine cuisine, while also learning culinary traditions from the West. The trip brought them from Shanghai to Suzhou, as well as Sichuan, Beijing, and Xi'an. Each city and province they visited had its own unique cuisine and flavors—and everywhere they went, they were treated to three multiple course meals per day.

In Shanghai, the group stayed in the famed Jing Jiang Hotel. The American chefs met with their Chinese counterparts at the hotel, teaching them the basics of how to cook an American breakfast that could be served to Western businessmen. Chef Jasper White remembers being served deep-fried eggs one day at breakfast, and then teaching the Chinese chefs how to pan-fry an egg. Chef Moncef Meddeb tried to show them how to make pastry, but flour was not available. That evening, they were invited to dine with the governor and mayor, Jiang Zemin, who later became the President of China. Their meal started in a dining room that was elaborately set

with special tools and dining utensils—the confused American diners soon realized that it was set up for them to enjoy hairy crab, one male and one female per person. After hairy crab, they moved to another table to enjoy the remainder of the courses, followed by a visit to the state theater. Their next stop was a quick visit to Suzhou, a city west of Shanghai, where they enjoyed the region's famed xiao long bao (soup dumplings). The food here was noticeably sweeter than in Shanghai. Following Suzhou, they made their way to Sichuan province, where they ate the most beautiful spicy regional food. And then they were off to their next stop, Beijing, where they were hosted at the state guest house, the Emperor's summer palace. It was like staying at a museum and the rules were incredibly strict—so strict, Sally stayed only two days, as it was completely isolated with no visitors or phone calls allowed. Their final destination was Xi'an, where they brought the chefs to visit the famous terracotta warriors and ate the local favorite: dumplings in every style imaginable.

While a very special experience for all the attendees, the biggest significance of this trip was the chefs' newfound knowledge of Chinese cuisine. Upon returning, Chef Moncef Meddeb shared details of what he learned on that epic trip with *The Boston Globe*. And Jasper White, now considered to be one of the earliest champions of New England cuisine, brought his new understanding of Chinese regional food back to his kitchen. "I realized you don't get a true sense of local food unless you're tasting seasonal and regional ingredients," Jasper recently shared with me. "I approached the entire concept of New England food differently after that." He also became fascinated with the concept of combinations after the trip, thinking about different ways to pair food and flavors. It was a trip that created ripples throughout the greater Boston dining scene for years to come.

SALLY WAS ENDLESSLY GRATEFUL for and attributed much of their success to the support from the community. She always wanted to give back in any way possible. Sally Ling's hosted many charity events, including campaign dinners for Governor Dukakis and catered James Beard dinners. Martin Yan visited whenever he was in the

area. Yo-Yo Ma and Julia Child were regulars, and Julia celebrated her eightieth birthday at Sally Ling's in 1992. I remember looking up at her, thinking she was so tall, not taking into account that I was only ten years old. (I later learned she was, in fact, very tall—no wonder why she towered over my dad!)

Even though my mom never had a formal culinary education, she loved to study cookbooks, travel the world to discover new ingredients and flavors, and create new dishes with their chefs. I remember seeing her face on the billboard on the Mass Pike as we drove into the city, realizing that perhaps she was not exactly a "normal mom." She taught alongside Julia Child in the Master Chef series at Boston University and looks back proudly on these amazing experiences.

My parents are the reason I'm here today, in more ways than one. My dad laid my foundation with his teachings and discipline and my mom is very much my muse. Together they created Sally Ling's and me, and I've made it my personal duty and responsibility to continue the family legacy (as good Chinese daughters should!). I embrace it with all my heart. I am grateful to them and all the hardships they endured. I appreciate how they lived their lives honestly; they were on the outside exactly who they were on the inside. Ultimately, they fought for their own happiness, which was also very instructive to me. I have the utmost pride in my parents, and sincerely hope I've made them proud as a daughter, a mother, and a restauranteur.

HOW TO USE THIS COOKBOOK

You've likely followed many recipes in your lifetime—but we've organized this book a bit differently, and wanted to tell you about it before you jump in.

When we started our Dumpling Daughter cooking classes during the pandemic, we learned how important it was to set our students up for success. In Chinese cuisine, the actual cooking happens fast and is often the last step. Before the cooking, you need to prepare: chopping vegetables, slicing and marinating meat, making different sauces. Because of this, we incorporated a Prep List into our recipes. In addition to the ingredients, this aims to help home cooks get everything ready to go before the oil hits the hot pan.

Next, here's how we approach serving sizes, and the overall approach to dinner. Chinese culture places a great deal of importance on balance, and we honor that through the food we put on our tables. Most recipes in this book yield about 4 servings. However, we're anticipating that you're making more than one dish per meal. We know it can be a tough sell to convince people to make multiple dishes from a cookbook on a busy weeknight, but here's how we approach it. On a typical weeknight at my house, I aim to serve a vegetable dish, a protein-focused dish, and either noodles or rice on the side. The good news is that you can get most of the prep done at any point in the day—this works to my advantage!

On a weeknight, this might look like:

Chicken with Celery & Carrots (pg. 226)

Scallion Lo Mein (pg. 156)

Napa Cabbage with Dried Shrimp (pg. 70)

Another great meal that my family loves:

Beef with Asparagus (pg. 109)

Baby Boy Choy with Fresh Garlic (pg. 167)

White rice

Here is another favorite (but simple) combination:

Jumbo Shrimp with Snow Peas (pg. 195)

Sally Ling's Fried Rice (pg. 128)

On a Friday night, I might feel up for making a bigger spread, adding a few appetizers—like dumplings (pg. 87) or scallion pancakes (pg. 163)—a braised meat, noodles, sautéed vegetables, soup, and a simple dessert.

When it's a dinner party, I really go for it. I typically plan to serve 4 to 5 appetizers, 2 meat dishes, 1 seafood dish, a noodle dish, a rice dish, soup, and a dessert. (Typically, I serve American desserts because that's what I love!) For more details on how to plan, make, and serve a banquet-style Chinese feast, see pg. 229. Because I love entertaining and making a multitude of dishes for friends and family, we dedicated a whole section on how to do so.

Last tip: These recipes aren't hard. If you follow the instructions and take your time to set up properly, you'll find that they come together quickly. I am honored to share my family's recipes with you!

STOCKING A CHINESE PANTRY

Soy Sauce

醬油 | jiàngyóu

Soy sauce was created 2,200 years ago during the Western Han dynasty and has been used abundantly throughout Asia since that time. Made from fermented soybeans, it is used across the globe today to add color, flavor, and umami to dishes. Soy sauce is great for cooking and for dipping alike.

Dark Soy Sauce

老抽 | lǎo chōu

Thicker, darker, and slightly sweeter than regular soy sauce, dark soy is a staple in Chinese cooking. Most often used to add more flavor and color, it is widely used in meat braises, such as our Soy Braised Pork Belly, Red-Cooked Pigs Feet, and Braised Beef Shank.

Light Soy Sauce

生抽 | jiàngyóu

Light soy sauce is used to add light salt to a dish. It doesn't add color to food as much as regular soy sauce does. It's great for adding mild flavor to stir-fry dishes, cold appetizers, and dipping sauces.

Oyster Sauce

蠔油 | háoyóu

Oyster sauce is made with oyster juices, salt, sugar, and is often thickened with a starch. This sauce is packed with flavor and is used in stir-fry dishes. Like soy sauce, oyster sauce adds a savory element to a dish, but it also adds a level of richness. Oyster sauce is a great addition to thicken meat fillings for wontons and dumplings.

Black Vinegar

黑醋 | hēi cù

Black vinegar is aged in clay pots, creating a unique, earthy flavor. It is less acidic than white vinegar, with different regions in China and Taiwan creating their own variations. Here in the U.S., Chinkiang is the most popular and accessible brand. Black vinegar is great for cooking and for making quick dipping sauces.

Shaoxing Rice Wine

绍兴酒 | shàoxīngjiǔ

Ten years ago, Shaoxing rice wine was not readily available, and people used sherry as a substitute. Today it's in every Asian market and can even be found in liquor stores. This wine is a staple ingredient in many Chinese dishes and will elevate your dish. Often, a small splash is all it takes to enhance the flavor. Generic rice wine can be found in the Asian aisle in most supermarkets at around 5% ABV. But if you want your food to taste authentic, you'll have to search harder for a higher ABV wine. We particularly love to use Shaoxing rice wine with seafood. When the wine goes into a hot wok, it sends an incredible aroma through a kitchen.

Rice Vinegar or Rice Wine Vinegar

米醋 | Mǐcù

This is an essential ingredient in our pantry. Rice vinegar delivers a mild acidity with a hint of sweetness.

Fish Sauce

魚露 | yú lù

Fish sauce is perhaps best-known as an ingredient in Pad Thai, but it can be utilized in many dishes to add saltiness and deep, complex flavors. Start by adding a small amount to taste.

Sesame Oil

芝麻油 | zhīmayóu

Sesame oil comes in both light and dark varieties. The light version is commonly used in dishes where its mild flavor won't overwhelm the dish. On the other hand, dark sesame oil uses toasted seeds, which provides a much stronger aroma and flavor. We generally prefer to use light sesame oil. A little bit goes a long way! We use it in cold dishes and as a finishing drizzle. (Beware: adding it too early in a stir-fry can make the dish bitter.)

Chili Oil

辣油 | làyóu

Chili oil is found on the tables of Chinese restaurants the way ketchup is waiting for you at a Western restaurant. Chili oil is a versatile addition and incredibly simple to make. Once you learn how, you'll be sure to always have it in stock at home. (See our version on pg. 45.)

Hoisin Sauce

海鲜酱 | hǎixiān jiàng

The name of this sauce in Chinese is derived from the word "seafood." While Hoisin sauce does not contain seafood, it's fragrant in a similar way and tends to be a sweet addition to a dish. We love it with Minced Chicken with Lettuce Leaves, Moo Shu, Peking Duck, Coco's Roll-Ups, and Taiwanese Buns. This thick sauce is also great to use when marinating meat for barbecue.

Sacha

沙茶 | shā chá

In my opinion, this is one the most underrated condiments on the planet. It is marketed as barbecue sauce, but it has nothing to do with grilling. What it does have is a one-of-a-kind flavor, lending a mild seafood, garlic, and spicy element to a dish. This hidden secret is great for stir-fries, rice bowls, and elevating dipping sauces.

XO Sauce

XO 醬 | XO jiàng

XO sauce is a relatively new ingredient, created in Hong Kong in the 1980s. The main ingredients are shrimp and scallops, making it an expensive luxury ingredient. However, because it features such bold flavors, you only need a little bit. It's sweet, salty, savory, and spicy, beguiling even the most seasoned taste buds. It is becoming more widely used by international chefs as they discover what a hidden gem it is.

Sesame Paste

芝麻酱 | zhīmajiàng

You might see sesame paste and think "tahini," but the Chinese have their own version made from toasted sesame seeds, making it darker in color and nuttier and stronger in taste. It is a staple in Chinese desserts and pastries. At Dumpling Daughter, we tend to use it in sauces, like as a base for our Dan Dan mien, or in place of peanut butter. As Dumpling Daughter is dedicated to being 100% nut free, we've found sesame paste to be a great alternative to nut butters.

Hot Bean Sauce

紅油辣豆瓣醬 | hóng yóu là dòubàn jiàng

One of the most important ingredients in Sichuan cooking, this sauce is made by fermenting bean paste with chili peppers. Salty, spicy, and bold in flavor, you can't have Mapo tofu without this sauce.

Chili Paste

辣醬 | làjiàng

In this book, when we say "chili paste," we are referring to any of your favorite spicy sauces. This can be Sriracha, Sambal Olek, or Dumpling Daughter Spicy Sweet Soy. The dishes that call for it don't need to be spicy, but if you like spice, go for it!

Sriracha

是拉差 | shì lā chà

Sriracha has become a household name in this country. Made from garlic and chili, it is believed that sriracha originated in Thailand. This is a go-to sauce for adding heat and can be bought in all major markets today. Here in the U.S., the most popular manufacturer is Huy Fong Foods—the one with the rooster!

Sweet Bean Paste

甜面酱 | tiánmiànjiàng

Sweet Bean Paste is a thick, dark, brown condiment popularly used in Northern China. The paste is both sweet and savory and adds a rich color to a dish. We use this paste in our Grandma's Beijing Meat Sauce, and while it looks like hoisin, it's not as sweet. In Beijing, they commonly serve it alongside fresh cucumber.

Chinese Sausage

腊肠 | làcháng

Chinese sausage is a preserved meat, making it the perfect protein to have on hand to add flavor when you need it. We look for a sausage that is both sweet and savory, and often add it to fried rice, congee, and noodle dishes. I especially love it in sautéed leafy greens, as it brings a ton of flavor and texture.

Dry Shiitake Mushroom

冬菇 | dōnggū

You'll find this ingredient in every Chinese pantry. These dried mushrooms are perfect for adding flavor and texture to hearty soups, slow-cooked meats, and stir-fried vegetables. Invest in a bag of dry shiitake—you won't regret it.

Wood Ear Mushrooms

木耳 | mù'ěr

These mushrooms are not as intimidating as their name might suggest. A staple in Chinese cuisine, they were named because they look like little ears growing on tree trunks. Used medicinally by Eastern cultures, these mushrooms are high in protein and iron, and low in calorie and fat content; they're also known to be good for lowering cholesterol. They are typically bought dry; once rehydrated, they are mild in flavor, slippery, crispy, and crunchy—and really delicious when tossed in a sesame soy dressing with chili oil.

Sichuan Pickled Mustard

榨菜 | zhàcài

This ingredient is made by fermenting the stem of the mustard plant. It is a combination of salty, sour, and spicy with a crunchy yet soft texture similar to pickles. Find it in Asian markets or online, packaged in cans or in vacuum-sealed packs.

Fermented Black Beans

豆豉 | dòuchǐ

Not to be confused with the dry black beans that you likely have in your pantry, these fermented soybeans add a ton of savory and earthy flavor to a dish. This ingredient is most commonly used in Cantonese cuisine and makes a great addition of complex flavor to slow-cooked and stir-fried dishes. They are typically sold at Asian markets or online and are worth seeking out.

Water Chestnuts

馬蹄 | mǎtí

Water chestnuts are not a nut, but rather a tuber that grows in freshwater. Virtually flavorless, they are used to add texture and crunch without altering anything else. They can be found in cans in the Asian section of almost any grocery store.

Preserved Mustard Greens

碎米芽菜 | suì mǐ yá cài

Do not confuse this with Sichuan pickled mustard, as this condiment is quite different. While both come from the same plant, preserved mustard greens are made by drying the stems, then fermenting them with salt and water, then boiling them with sugar, and then fermenting them again with spices. By fermenting twice, this ingredient possesses a unique, crunchy texture and flavor. Get creative and add it on different dishes, even your breakfast eggs!

Fish Balls

魚丸 | yú wán

I like to call fish balls "hot dogs of the sea." They are made from fish paste that is shaped into a ball, resulting in a tight texture similar to a hot dog. There are many types of fish balls—depending on the region, there are variations in the type of fish used, the seasonings, and the use of other ingredients. When I was little, I would stab them and blow on them until they were cool, then enjoy them off the chopstick, like skewer food. In Asia, they are sold on the street like a hot dog in New York City.

Chinese Dates

紅棗 | hóngzǎo

Chinese dates are small, round, bright red fruits with a tight wrinkly skin. They are sweet and chewy and used in many Chinese desserts. They are also used to regulate sleep and reduce anxiety.

Medjool Dates

甜枣 | tián zǎo

While most people associate red dates with Chinese cuisine, I love to cook with Medjool Dates for their size and sweetness. They also make a great vegetarian option for fried rice, mimicking the commonly used Chinese sausage, adding a touch of sweetness to the dish as well as vitamins and nutrients—sneak some in for kids!

Dried Shrimp

蝦米 | xiāmi

Sun-drying shrimp is a historic method of preservation. Dried shrimp are commonly used in soup and sautéed vegetables to add savory and complex flavors. Today, dried shrimp is often given as a gift—the drying process makes them more expensive than fresh seafood. If you're entertaining, elevate the meal by adding dried seafood to your dish.

Star Anise

八角 | bājiǎo

Closely related to anise, star anise is a critical spice in Chinese cooking. It is one of the five spices in five spice powder and is an essential addition to any braise. Plus, it makes your house smell absolutely incredible.

Dry Sichuan Peppers

紅辣椒干 | hóng làjiāo gàn

We use these chilis to drive the heat in our homemade chili oil, but they are great for stir-fry dishes as well. The cooking process will extract their heat, and their size allows you to easily remove them before serving the dish. (Don't let that stop you from eating them whole—if you dare!) Before using the dried peppers in a stir-fry, soak them in water to rehydrate them first—this will awaken the spice.

Korean Chili Pepper Fine (Gochugaru)

辣椒粉 | làjiāo fěn

This spice is best-known for making kimchi, but its capabilities stretch far beyond that. The heat from this pepper is on the milder side and adds a smokiness that can transform the way you think about chili. Don't be surprised if you find yourself making chili oil just to infuse your kitchen with this aroma.

Chinese Cinnamon Stick

桂枝 | guì zhī

The cinnamon used in Chinese cooking is quite different than the cinnamon regularly found in Western cuisine. Both come from species of trees in the Laurel family, but Chinese cinnamon is much milder and more delicate in flavor, while also physically thicker and coarser in texture. Chinese cinnamon is usually used in savory dishes, whereas Americans tend to associate cinnamon with desserts. If you can't find Chinese cinnamon, you can substitute with regular cinnamon sticks—just use half the amount.

Five Spice Powder

五香粉 | wǔxiāng fěn

A seasoning commonly made from cinnamon, fennel seed, star anise, cloves, and pepper. Consider this spice a powerhouse, adding all five flavors to a dish. It's especially delicious on our Crispy Fried Chicken.

Umami Mushroom Seasoning

日式蘑菇调味 | rì shì mógū tiáowèi liào

Umami mushroom seasoning is a great item to add meaty, savory flavor for vegans and vegetarians. Where we might use seafood-based sauces to add this same flavor, umami mushroom seasoning is a great alternative for dietary restrictions.

Rock Candy (or Rock Sugar)

冰糖 | bīngtáng

Rock candy is the crystallized juice from sugarcane. You can find this special sugar in Asian markets or online. Rock candy creates a beautiful coating on meat, such as our Soy Braised Pork Belly and Red-Cooked Pigs Feet, that makes the dish shine—literally. In a pinch, use regular sugar in its place, but we urge you to try to find it!

Osmanthus Flower Syrup

桂花醬 | guìhuā jiàng

This thick syrup has a sweet, floral flavor, with a musky undernote and is commonly used in traditional Chinese desserts. We love how it dresses up our Chinese New Year Sweet Rice Cake.

Sweet Rice Flour

糯米粉 | nuòmǐfěn

Sometimes referred to as glutinous rice flour, this is a high-starch flour with a neutral flavor that is great as a thickening agent and for making desserts. Caution: this is not the same as regular rice flour, as they come from different plants. Look for the words "sweet" or "glutinous"—this will indicate that you've found the right product.

Potato/Tapioca Starch

番薯粉 | fānshǔ fěn

Potato and tapioca starch are great gluten-free thickening agents. Due to the increasing prevalence of gluten-free diets, these are now easy to find in most grocery stores.

Thousand-Year Egg

皮蛋 | pídàn

Also known as a preserved egg, this ingredient takes months to prepare, which is considerably less than the name would have you believe. Encased in a translucent, black, jelly-like texture, thousand-year eggs are perfectly salty with a rich, creamy yolk and a dark jade coloring. If you are partial to French blue cheese, you will love thousand-year eggs! This is one of my childhood favorites.

Wonton Skins

云吞皮 | yún tūn pí

Wonton skins can be found in the refrigerator section in almost all large grocery stores and in every Asian grocery store. Any brand will work fine for our recipes.

Spring Roll Skin

春卷皮 | chūnjuǎn pí

Delicate, handmade spring roll skins used to be sold at street markets in Asia. Today, they're machine-made in factories in Asia and the United States. These ready-made options are quite convenient and easy to use. Look for a square, wheat-based skin. (The circular rice-based skin used for summer rolls will not work for spring rolls.)

Firm Tofu

老豆腐 | lǎo dòufu

Firm tofu is the most widely available tofu in supermarkets. It is an incredibly versatile ingredient: it can be cut in different sizes and shapes to be pan-seared, sautéed, braised, or added to soup. A great introduction to those who may be wary about venturing into the world of tofu.

Soft Tofu

嫩豆腐 | nèn dòufu

Soft tofu retains the most water of all tofu types, giving it a mild flavor and creamy mouthfeel. It is also very delicate to the touch, so be careful when handling it, as it can crumble into small pieces. Soft tofu is perfect for making Mapo, as the tofu is merely a pleasant vehicle for the delicious and distinctive sauce.

Five Spice Tofu

豆腐干 | dòufu gān

Five Spice Tofu is made by marinating, braising, and baking firm tofu with five spice seasoning, resulting in a flavor-packed tofu that is dense enough to stir-fry without crumbling. It is a very popular vegan ingredient, as it's a great stand-in for meat. If you can't find five spice tofu, look for other baked firm tofu options as a close substitute.

1

2

3

4

5

6

7

NOODLE TYPES

1 Bean Thread Vermicelli (or noodles)
粉丝 | fěnsī

Bean thread noodles are a type of Asian cellophane noodle from mung bean starch. These look very similar to fine rice noodles, with both being a pale white color and very thin in diameter. The difference is that bean thread noodles are a bit smoother, whereas rice noodles tend to be slightly stickier. These can definitely be confusing at a grocery store, as they are often mislabeled. When in doubt, check for mung bean on the ingredient list.

2 Rice Cakes
年糕 | niángāo

Rice Cakes are usually found in the refrigerated sections of Asian grocery stores (next to fresh noodles), in vacuum-sealed bags. These are similar to Korean Tteobokki in texture but vary in size. Their thin oval shape holds a sauce well.

3 White Noodles
白麵 | báimiàn

What we refer to as "white noodles" are simply Chinese wheat-based noodles that are similar in shape and size to spaghetti. These noodles are intended to be thicker than the other noodle types. Don't stress if you can't find the exact noodle we recommend. Just look out for those key qualities and you'll be sure to enjoy the dish.

4 Egg Noodles
蛋麵 | dàn miàn

Nine times out of ten, Chinese stir-fry noodle dishes will use a type of egg noodle. There is a huge range of Chinese egg noodles out there, but almost all of them will work for our recipes. We prefer and recommend noodles on the thinner side, but wavy, like ramen. The wavy shape provides texture for sauces to cling to, and the thinness provides a nice balance.

5 Italian Pasta
義大利麵 | yìdàlì miàn

I love mixing cuisines, but most importantly, Italian pasta is a great vehicle for delicious, rich sauces. I do not discriminate on noodles! When I'm making Chinese dishes with Italian pasta, I use long, cylindrical pastas, like spaghetti, linguine, or bucatini, because they hold sauce so beautifully. When I feed my boys, I like to serve rotelle, penne rigate, and fusilli—the fun shapes are an excellent vehicle for hearty meat sauces.

6 Rice Noodle Vermicelli
米粉 | mǐfěn

Rice noodle and bean thread vermicelli are almost like adopted children: they share a name and have similar characteristics but come from different parents. Rice noodles are the parent to rice vermicelli as opposed to cellophane noodles being the parent to bean thread vermicelli. Again, when in doubt, look for rice starch on the ingredient list.

7 Dangmyeon (Japchae) Noodles
韩国粉丝 | hánguó fěnsī

These are Korean noodles, sometimes referred to as glass noodles, made from sweet potato starch (and are gluten free!). These fall under a larger category of cellophane noodles. I love to experiment with mixing different cuisines, and these noodles have a unique chewy, slippery texture that is unlike its Chinese cousins.

KNIFE SKILLS AND TECHNIQUES

The most beautiful and delicious Chinese food comes from a delicate approach. Everything that goes into the dish should be treated with finesse. Excellent Chinese food comes from the quality of the ingredients, the style in which everything is prepared, and the amount of time and temperature applied during cooking; if these metrics are met from start to finish, you will have a dish that will "pass with flying colors" as my dad would say! Following the cutting techniques closely will ensure an authentic Chinese dish, in appearance and taste, as the recommended cooking times and temperatures are based on accurate cuts.

The Chinese cleaver is a beautiful tool. Accomplished chefs love their collection of knives, but the Chinese chef only needs one, the Chinese cleaver. A Chinese cleaver can perform the most delicate cuts but can also be used to butcher a whole chicken. This all depends on the skills of the chef. The cleaver can be sharpened with a simple stone—or as my mom does, swiped across the back of a plate with a rough edge. Always be sure to cut with a sharp knife!

When cutting, always hold the handle of the knife in your dominant hand with a relaxed, but firm grip. Slide your hand forward so that your thumb and index finger have full control over the knife. With your other hand, hold down the food you're cutting, with your fingers curved down and inward to reveal only your knuckles, so as not to slip and cut your fingertips. The knuckles are your guide, and the cleaver should rest against the knuckles as the neutral position. Always make sure to keep the knuckles closest to the knife and never raise your knife higher than your non-dominant hand.

A great tip on cutting—I like to cut vegetables before meat, so I don't have to wash my cutting board an extra time! This requires some extra planning but will save time when executing your meal.

MEATS

Sliced

When slicing meats, hold the meat firmly on the cutting board with your knuckles curled and perpendicular to your knife. Cut straight down into slices with a back-and-forth motion.

Shredded or Slivers

Slivers or shredded meat is the most common cut in Chinese cooking, because it showcases refined knife skills. Similar to a julienne cut, the goal is to cut the meat into uniform thin strips.

Begin by slicing the item into flat, thin slices. Special note: if you're cutting flank steak, be sure to cut across the grain—the grain references the direction the muscle fibers run. Cutting across the grain shortens the fibers and makes the meat more tender and easier to chew.

Then, stack the slices and cut through the stack to create thin strips. To achieve a longer length, cut on a diagonal, the greater the angle, the longer the length of the final product. To achieve a shorter length, cut more perpendicularly to the strips.

Cubed

Cubing comes after slicing. The size of these cubes are determined by the thickness of the slices. Cut the meat into slices that are as thick as the desired cube. Then, lay the slices flat and cut into equally thick strips. Rotate the strips 90 degrees and cut across the strips to make even cubes.

Slant Slice

When slant slicing, hold the meat firmly on the cutting board with your free hand. Angle the knife almost parallel to the board and slice with a back-and-forth motion to achieve thin slices.

VEGETABLE CUTS

1 Bias

Cutting on a bias is a knife cut at an angle, typically 45 degrees. A bias cut adds visual appeal to the dish and more surface area on the vegetable for browning and reducing cooking time.

2 Sliced

When slicing vegetables, hold the vegetables firmly on the cutting board with your knuckles curled and perpendicular to your knife. Cut straight down into slices.

3 Julienne

Matchstick, or julienne, is a knife cut that produces a long thin strip, similar to a matchstick. Begin by thinly slicing the vegetable about ¼ inch thick. Then lay the sliced vegetable flat and cut into thin strips, about ¼ inch thick.

4 Baton

When cutting cucumber batons, cut the cucumber into 3-inch long cylinders. Slice each cylinder in half lengthwise. Then, slice each half lengthwise into three equal sized batons. This baton is the perfect size to retain a crunch through the pickling process.

5 Wedge

This cut is used for spherical vegetables. Cut the vegetable in half vertically, then place each half cut side up. Cut each half into 3 to 4 wedges, similar to an orange wedge. Then, cut each wedge in half horizontally.

6 Diced

Diced vegetables are similar to chopped vegetables in that you want even pieces, but tend to be a bit larger, usually ½ to 1 inch pieces. Slice your vegetables into strips then rotate the strips 90 degrees, line up the ends, and cut into even pieces.

7 Oblique

An oblique cut, also known as a roll cut, is used to cut long vegetables, such as Chinese eggplant and daikon. This is a beautiful cut very common in Chinese cuisine. Hold the vegetable with your free hand and cut diagonally at the tip. Then, roll the vegetable a quarter turn and cut again at the same angle. Not every piece will be the same shape, but they should be the same size. Continue to cut and roll until you reach the other end of the vegetable.

8 Chopped

This cut requires chopping vegetables into small pieces. Chopped vegetables are slightly larger than minced, such as chopped scallions used to garnish many dishes.

9 Minced

Mincing comes from chopping the vegetable, then continuing to chop into smaller pieces. When I mince, I constantly move my food into tight small piles and chop quickly to mince in a speedy manner. Finely minced ingredients allow even distribution of flavor throughout a dish, such as the ginger in dumpling filling.

10 Sliced Lengthwise

We often use this cut when a vegetable is too thick. In the case of scallions, the white root ends are more spicy, so we slice thicker ends in half lengthwise before chopping to achieve smaller pieces.

11 Cilantro Garnish

To bring the best out of your cilantro, soak in ice water for 30 minutes, then drain and pat dry. Carefully pick the leaves off the stem. The stems have great flavor and can be minced for another dish!

10 & 2 Sliced Scallions

This is a very popular style of cutting scallions in Chinese cooking. Start by slicing lengthwise (10) and then slicing into desired length (2).

LAYING A FOUNDATION

Building Blocks for Chinese Cuisine—
and Life in General

Classic Braised Beef Shank

From Scratch Chicken Broth

Vegetable Broth

Perfect Dumpling Sauce

Gourmet Duck Sauce

Sesame Sauce

Dumpling Daughter Red Chili Oil

Peppercorn Oil

Perfect Soft Egg with Soy Sauce

Mom's Marbled Tea Eggs

MY FATHER WAS A RATHER INTIMIDATING MAN, with amazing posture and a deep, commanding voice. He was incredibly cool, always wearing tinted glasses and a perfect suit, often with an ascot or a pocket square. He smoked cigarettes and an old pipe; his presence demanded attention when he walked in a room. I was always somewhat in awe of him and his seemingly endless wisdom. And while so many of the recipes in this cookbook come from my mother and her restaurants, much of the foundation for my cooking education starts with my father.

My dad was born in Nanjing during the second Sino-Japanese War and grew up during World War II. He and his family fled their home to escape from the Japanese, moving fourteen times in thirteen years. Their lives were hard: his family of seven received one egg per week, and it would always go to my Uncle Clifford—he was the youngest and needed the protein the most. Later in life, my father considered eggs to be extremely special, and he remarked that having a dozen eggs in the refrigerator was a true luxury. Because of him, whenever I make a recipe that calls for egg whites, I make sure to use the yolk for something else. I can never waste an egg. (Or a blank piece of paper. Turns out paper was also nearly impossible to come by in his early years.) Today, I realize that it was the scarcity of almost everything that made him appreciate living life to the fullest.

From a very early age, my father encouraged me to analyze everything, big or small. He explained that in life we must analyze situations, ideas, products, people, relationships, decisions, and if we do this, then we will make smarter decisions. I realize now that this lesson is the foundation of everything I learned from my father.

When I was in the eighth grade, my dad asked me to start making family dinner each Sunday night. I was struck with anxiety—up until this point, my repertoire included instant ramen, Kraft macaroni and cheese, and ziti with jarred tomato sauce. I loved cooking Italian food because I felt like I had easy access to great Chinese food any time I wanted it. So that's where I began, with a jar of tomato sauce and a box of pasta. I decided to enhance the dish with some sautéed onions, but promptly scorched them in the searing hot pan. I

continued, adding the sauce, expecting the blackened onions to add flavor. They added flavor alright—but they also made the dinner inedible. I analyzed my mistakes, and tried again the next week, gently sautéing the onions and adding fresh basil at the end. This time, both my dad and little sister gave me a thumbs up.

My best friend, Carla, was Italian. When she heard about my adventures with home cooking, she told me that her dad cooked sauce from scratch. I was shocked. Italian people made their own sauce from fresh tomatoes? I had no idea that was even possible! I began to experiment, learning to go low and slow and reduce ingredients for more flavor. One night, Carla's dad made us linguine with pesto. I was floored. I'd never tasted anything like it, and I knew I had to recreate it at home. The very next day, I bought a blender from the Walgreens next to Sally Ling's in Newton. That Sunday, when my dad took a bite of my pesto dish, he gave me a huge smile and a

My father always encouraged me to think about how to lay the best foundation for my life. "A happy life is like a house or a building," he wrote to me in a letter. "It needs a solid foundation."

nod of approval. Tapping the side of the dish with his chopsticks, he gave me his assessment; he preferred red sauce but loved how I was trying new things. With his encouragement, I was inspired to learn more and more.

For me, this was the perfect way to learn to cook. My father was always honest with me, and together, we'd analyze my choices and talk about ways to improve. We continued these cooking classes over the years. They brought us a lot of joy, togetherness, and truly delicious food.

My father always encouraged me to think about how to lay the best foundation for my life. "A happy life is like a house or a building," he wrote to me in a letter. "It needs a solid foundation." Likewise, in Chinese cooking, one must build that strong foundation with building blocks of flavor. The recipes in this chapter, whether they are restorative broths or special sauces to make your food sing, are the recipes we use again and again.

CLASSIC BRAISED BEEF SHANK

紅燒牛健 **Yields approximately 6 shanks and 8 cups of beef broth**

This recipe is a real workhorse. Not only does it provide lots of braised beef that can be used to make our famous Coco's Roll-Ups (pg. 159), but it also provides flavorful beef broth perfect for a rich and cozy beef noodle soup when you need it most. I often describe this as charcuterie without the curing process because you can eat it sliced as a cold appetizer or add it to your sandwich. I once added beef shank to an all-American grilled cheese, and everyone agreed it was a fabulous idea. This recipe requires an overnight braise, but afterward you'll have delicious meat for days.

Don't be deterred by the cut—it's similar to the meat used in Osso Bucco. The cut is translated from Chinese to English as "beef shank" which is how I grew up referring to it. However, most butchers can get their hands on it if you ask for "beef heel" muscle, which is the most accurate name for the authentic recipe.

4 to 4½ pounds beef shank
(about 6 shanks)

2-inch piece fresh ginger root,
peeled and roughly chopped
into 4 pieces

½ cup rock candy or yellow
rock sugar

4 pieces star anise

1 cinnamon stick

5 cloves

½ teaspoon fennel seeds

4 bay leaves

1 teaspoon salt

2 tablespoons soy sauce

4 tablespoons dark soy sauce

1 cup Shaoxing rice wine

Braising

Place the beef shank in a large stock pot and cover with water. Over high heat, bring the pot to a boil. When grayish foam rises to the top, remove from heat and pour out water. (This will remove any impurities from the protein and ensure the best flavor.) Rinse the beef and wash the pot, then return the beef to the clean pot.

Add the remaining ingredients to the pot and fill with water until the beef is submerged.

Bring to a boil over high heat, then reduce heat to medium-low. Partially cover the pot and simmer gently for about 1 to 1½ hours. Check for doneness by poking the beef with a chopstick or fork; if you can puncture the beef effortlessly, it is done. Poke holes all over the shanks, allowing the braise to saturate the beef. Let the beef marinate overnight in the refrigerator.

The next day, remove the beef shanks from the braising liquid and wrap tightly with plastic wrap. Sieve the spices from the braising liquid and reserve; it can be used to make beef broth, which will keep in the freezer for up to 3 months (pg. 180).

Freeze the shanks to use as needed. Keep in mind, the beef is easiest to slice when it's partially frozen.

FROM SCRATCH CHICKEN BROTH

 Yields about 2 quarts

There's nothing like a house filled with the aroma of simmering chicken broth. This is a basic chicken bone broth that can be used for noodle soup, wonton soup, or simply enjoyed by itself.

In Chinese cuisine, chicken soup is known as a dish to help strengthen and soothe the body. This recipe is the perfect remedy for those who aren't feeling well, are recovering from surgery, or for postpartum women.

3 to 5 pound whole chicken

1-inch piece fresh ginger root, peeled and roughly chopped

1 tablespoon salt, plus more to taste

Cooking

Remove and discard the skin from the chicken. Cut the breasts from the bone and wrap it for later use in another dish. We don't like food waste!

Place the chicken and the ginger into a medium-sized pot. Add enough water to submerge the chicken by about an inch. Cover the pot and bring to a boil over high heat, then reduce heat to low and simmer for 2 hours, partially uncovering the pot.

Remove from heat and let cool at room temperature or in the refrigerator. I like to refrigerate it overnight so the fat rises to the top and solidifies. Skim the fat and discard. Strain the broth into a pot and discard the chicken. Taste and season with salt. If you're not using it right away, the broth can be frozen for up to 3 months.

VEGETABLE BROTH

素菜湯 **Yields about 2 quarts**

At the restaurant we offer beef, chicken, and vegetable broths as the base for our noodles in order to accommodate all eaters. Here's how we make our vegetable broth so you can do the same.

1 big handful soybean sprouts, rinsed

2 stalks celery, chopped into 2-inch pieces

½ yellow onion, chopped into 3 wedges

1 medium tomato, chopped into 4 wedges

1 carrot, peeled and chopped into 2-inch pieces

1 tablespoon umami mushroom seasoning

Salt to taste

Cooking

Put the vegetables and 10 cups of water into a 6-quart pot. Bring to a boil over high heat and add the mushroom seasoning. Stir, reduce the heat to low, partially cover the pot with a lid, and simmer for 2 hours.

Strain the broth and discard the vegetables. Taste and season with salt. If you're not using it right away, this broth can be frozen for up to 3 months.

PERFECT DUMPLING SAUCE

餃子汁　**Yields about ¾ cup, about 4 to 6 servings**

Savory with a kick, this homemade sauce is the perfect complement to dumplings. We use our Dumpling Daughter Red Chili Oil (pg. 45) here, but red chili paste or even sriracha will do the trick. The fresh garnish really brings it home.

Garnishes

1-inch piece fresh ginger root, peeled and finely minced

1 scallion, trimmed and finely minced

4 stems cilantro (optional or to taste), finely chopped

Sauce

½ cup soy sauce

¼ cup sugar

¼ cup black vinegar

1½ tablespoons Dumpling Daughter Red Chili Oil (optional), pg. 45

2 teaspoons sesame oil

Mix

Add the sauce ingredients to a medium bowl and whisk until the sugar has dissolved. If you like things spicy, add the Dumpling Daughter Red Chili Oil or the chili paste. Add the garnishes, mix, and serve alongside dumplings.

GOURMET DUCK SAUCE

苏梅酱 **Yields approximately 1 cup**

This is something I'll make on the fly when I need the sticky, sweet flavors to complement crispy appetizers. It's a must for Sally Ling's Spring Rolls (pg. 79)!

½ cup apricot preserves

½ cup apple sauce

3 tablespoons white vinegar

2 tablespoons sugar

Add the ingredients to a medium bowl and whisk until smooth.

SESAME SAUCE

芝麻酱 **Yields 2 cups**

In this cookbook, we call for this sauce in a number of recipes: Cold Noodles with Sesame Sauce (pg. 113), Sesame Wontons (pg. 174), and Dan Dan Mien (pg. 171). But honestly, it's a great sauce to put on grilled meat, or to use as a dip for grilled or raw vegetables.

¾ cup sesame paste

½ cup vegetable oil

½ cup soy sauce

¼ cup black vinegar

⅓ cup sugar

2 tablespoons Peppercorn
  Oil, pg. 46

1 tablespoon chili oil

In a medium bowl, combine the ingredients and blend with an immersion blender until smooth. This sauce can also be made in a food processor, a blender, or whisked by hand. It will keep in the refrigerator for up to 6 months.

DUMPLING DAUGHTER RED CHILI OIL

本楼紅油 **Yields about 2½ cups**

This might sound crazy, but there is nothing like this chili oil on the market. It's a rich, luxe oil for drizzling, and our take on the trademark ingredient of Sichuan food, which relies heavily on red chili oil for the texture, color, and spice. Unlike commercial red chili oil, we don't use peppercorn, but rather combine three peppers hailing from different cultures: Korean, American, and Chinese. With its vibrant color, strong aroma (not to mention how wonderful your kitchen will smell after you make it), and the mildly spicy sensation it brings to your food, you'll be thrilled to have it on hand.

¾ cup gochugaru Korean chili pepper powder, finely ground

2 tablespoons red chili pepper flakes

10 dried Sichuan chili peppers

3 cups vegetable oil

Place the chili powder, the pepper flakes, and the chili peppers in a heatproof bowl or pot. In a separate heavy-bottomed pot, heat the vegetable oil over high heat for about 4 minutes, or until it reaches 375°F. The oil must not get hotter than 390°F.

Pour the oil into the bowl with the chili peppers. You should hear a sizzling sound and smell a beautiful aroma. If you don't hear a sizzling sound, then your oil is not hot enough.

Carefully mix the pepper and oil, making sure none splashes out of the bowl. Let sit for 30 minutes, mix again, then let sit for another 30 minutes and mix one more time. Do not cover the oil until it has fully cooled. The oil can sit at room temperature for up to 12 hours. Once the mixture has rested, the peppers will sink to the bottom. Don't agitate the peppers before straining it—allow them to rest at the bottom of the pot. Carefully pour the oil through a fine mesh sieve into a clean container for storage. Dispose of the residual powder at the bottom.

Like most oils, this can be kept in your pantry or refrigerator for up to 6 months. When you use the oil, be sure not to dip dirty utensils into it, as this will make it go bad.

PEPPERCORN OIL

花椒油 **Yields ¾ cup**

Sichuan peppercorn oil is something you can buy in a store or online, but we love to make our own at home. This oil will give your food that distinctive ma-la flavor—slightly floral and a bit tingly—that makes Sichuan food so addictive.

¾ cup canola or vegetable oil

¼ cup Sichuan peppercorns

Place the oil in a medium pan and heat over medium-high until it reaches 350°F. The oil should shimmer but not smoke.

Meanwhile, heat a separate medium pan over high heat until hot but not smoking, about 20 to 30 seconds. Add the peppercorns to the pan and reduce heat to medium. Toast the peppercorns for about 20 seconds, shaking the pan to keep them moving. After the peppercorns are toasted, crush them with a wooden spoon. Remove from heat and transfer the peppercorns to a medium-sized, heatproof bowl.

Once the oil reaches 350°F, pour about 1 teaspoon over the peppercorns. The oil should begin fizzing immediately and release a spicy aroma. If the oil does not fizz, return the oil to the stove and continue heating. Continue testing and reheating as needed. When the oil is the correct temperature, pour it over the peppercorns. Let the peppercorns steep until the oil has cooled completely. Strain the oil into a clear container and discard the peppercorns.

Like most oils, this can be kept in your pantry or refrigerator for up to 6 months. When you use the oil, be sure not to dip dirty utensils into it, as this will make it go bad.

PERFECT SOFT EGG WITH SOY SAUCE

糖心蛋 **Yields 2 eggs**

Here's a different egg preparation to use as a topping for noodles, rice, and congee—or simply to eat on its own. My son Julian loves to break the egg and watch the yolk ooze out. There's a reason I call it perfect.

2 large eggs

½ teaspoon sugar

1 teaspoon oyster sauce

1 teaspoon soy sauce

Cooking

In a small pot, bring 2½ cups of water to a boil. Carefully place the eggs in the boiling water with a slotted spoon. Cook over high heat for 6 minutes.

To the bowl you will serve the eggs in, add the sugar and 1 teaspoon of the boiling water used to cook the eggs. Mix to dissolve the sugar. Add the oyster sauce and the soy sauce and mix well.

When the eggs have boiled for 6 minutes, carefully transfer the pot to the sink and run cold water on the eggs for 20 seconds. Let the eggs cool in the water for 5 minutes.

Carefully peel the eggs, drop in the bowl of sauce, and enjoy.

MOM'S MARBLED TEA EGGS

媽咪茶葉蛋　**Yields 12 eggs**

These eggs bring me right back to childhood. My mom always had them on hand for a snack or breakfast. Today, I have them ready in the fridge to add some quick protein to any dish. They are the perfect addition to any noodle or rice bowl, or as a side for congee. Give them a try—you'll love them too!

1 dozen large eggs

½ cup oolong tea leaves
　(or 10 Lipton tea bags)

5 pieces star anise

1 tablespoon dark soy sauce

2 tablespoons soy sauce

In a medium-sized pot, bring enough water to cover the eggs (approximately 6 cups) to a boil over high heat. Carefully place the eggs into the boiling water with a slotted spoon—be careful not to crack them!

Boil for about 7 minutes, then remove the pot from the heat. Using a slotted spoon, transfer the eggs to an ice bath.

Add the remaining ingredients to the hot water in the pot to create a marinade and set aside.

When the eggs are cool enough to handle, hit each egg with the back of a spoon to create cracks across the shell, then carefully lower the eggs one by one into the marinade. It should still be warm.

Return the pot to low heat and cook for 1 hour. Remove from heat and leave the eggs in the marinade overnight in the refrigerator.

The next day, warm the eggs and marinade over low heat and serve warm or at room temperature.

If not eating within 24 hours, remove the eggs from the marinade; they will become salty if they sit too long. The marinated eggs can be kept in the refrigerator for up to 3 days.

THE KIDS' TABLE

My Favorite Childhood Dishes from
Family Restaurants and our Home Kitchen

Chinese New Year Sweet Rice Cake

Crystal Shrimp

Dad's Favorite Lion's Head
with Napa Cabbage

Sally Ling's Imperial Chicken

Sunday Congee

Minced Chicken with Lettuce Leaves

Classic Napa Cabbage with Dried Shrimp

Lobster Two Ways:

Sally Ling's Lobster with Ginger & Scallions

Lobster Cantonese Style

Grandpa's Red-Cooked Pigs Feet

Sally Ling's Vegetable Spring Rolls

Simple Sparerib & Daikon Soup

Handmade Wontons

Sally Ling's Wonton Soup

Homemade Dumplings:

Mom's Dumpling Dough

Pork & Cabbage Dumplings

Pork & Chive Dumplings

Chicken & Cabbage Dumplings

MY EARLIEST MEMORIES ARE OF BEING DIFFERENT. My father's rule was that we could not speak English in the house, only Chinese. I spent much of my day with my nanny, who only spoke Mandarin. We lived in Weston, Massachusetts, a predominantly white town. Not speaking English made my pre-school and early elementary school years painfully uncomfortable. I was incredibly shy and dreaded going to school, particularly getting on the bus. I hated feeling like everyone was looking at me—I'd scurry up the stairs, sit in the first seat, and slide over to the window. At school, I was made fun of for being Chinese. A popular bully would pull his eyes back and say "Ching ching chong chong, can you even see?" Or, "Do you know how to play chopsticks on the piano?" My shyness and lack of English made it impossible to stand up for myself.

I cried to my dad and told him I didn't want to go to school because I was made fun of for being Chinese. It feels like yesterday when my dad plopped me on the kitchen counter and looked me in the eye, telling me: "You are different, you are special, and one day you will use this to your advantage. Just watch, and remember what I say."

Throughout my childhood, my family took trips to places like Taiwan, Europe, and Tokyo. I returned with the best stuff—including a fancy Japanese lunchbox adorned with Hello Kitty. The Japanese made everything with such attention to detail: there was a compartment for everything, and even an eject button for chopsticks. (When you pressed it, the Hello Kitty pink chopsticks would shoot out of the side. Genius!) I remember thinking this was the height of coolness and appreciated that it was different from the standard Rainbow Brite American lunch boxes. At the lunch

table, the kids would stare out of the corners of their eyes, taking me in. They ate peanut butter and jelly sandwiches; I had rice with pickled cucumber, shredded pork and tofu. I used my chopsticks; they used their hands. I kept my head down and enjoyed my food, always remembering that my dad told me to be proud of my differences. It became easier over the years—I would think to myself: "So what, I'm different? No big deal." But despite my brave face, feeling like everyone's eyes were on me was something I continued to fear and struggle with over the years.

In those early years, my life was completely focused on school, skating, and dinners. I first stepped on the ice at the Babson Skating Center when I was six years old. I was nervous and terrified to have people watch me. My mom joined me on the ice, learning alongside me, and I finally began to feel comfortable. I loved the music and the feeling of freedom I experienced while skating, and my confidence grew as I learned. Skating soon became a huge focus for me, training six days a week with a nationally renowned coach at the Skating Club of Boston. My mom picked me up early from school every day, handing me two steamed buns or a bowl of noodles in a to-go box. This little routine anchored me and connected me to home each day.

Everyone in school knew me as the figure skater, which gave me great confidence. Soon, we began to choreograph programs, and my mom started to make me competition and practice dresses. (Whenever the other girls complimented my skating clothes, I was always so proud to tell them that my mom had made them.) I earned a spot performing my routine at the Babson Skating Club's annual skating show, which had never been granted to a minor before. I took my skating very seriously, and my hard work was being rewarded with increasingly larger roles. My parents were proud of me, which of course made me want to work even harder. Skating made me a more competitive person. I was finally coming out of my shell.

When I wasn't skating, it felt like my life revolved around food, restaurants, and family. One of my earliest memories of dining out was eating Beijing noodle soup at my mom's restaurant, Peking Cuisine, in Chinatown. I remember one of the waiters used to comment on how such a little girl could eat such a big bowl of noodles. It made me feel a little insecure because he said it so loudly, but I ate every last drop. I may have been shy, but I never cared about how people judged my appetite. I loved to eat!

When my parents opened Sally Ling's, it was entirely different. It was so fancy there: everyone wore tuxedos, suits, and beautiful dresses. I had to dress up in my best clothes, and upon walking in, I was always greeted by the general manager or the host. As I made my way to the table, every waiter said hello. I brought my Barbies and coloring books to keep myself entertained, though I would also look around and take it all in. I was always curious about what the adults were drinking in their fancy glassware and would sometimes sneak a sip of my mom's drink when she wasn't looking. (I'm guessing this is where my love of White Russians comes from.) Dinner always ended with me sitting on my mom's lap, my face nuzzled in her neck as she sat and talked with the adults. My dad would carry me down to the car and I would sleep all the way home and be carried into bed. Restaurant life was fancy, and every weekend was a party.

My parents were soon running several restaurants in the Boston area. There was the fancy new Sally Ling's at the Hyatt Regency; a more casual, family-oriented Sally Ling's in Newton Centre; an American restaurant called Boston Lobster House (at the original waterfront location of Sally Ling's); a fast casual restaurant called Sally's Wok in Marlborough; and an East-meets-West restaurant in Dedham called Sally's Pippins. My Aunt Wilma and Uncle Rick had several restaurants too, and we would go out to dinner with them and my cousins almost every week-

end. Whether it was one of our restaurants, theirs, or other restaurants in the Back Bay or the North End, it was almost always a white-tablecloth affair.

Going to Sally Ling's at the Hyatt Regency was particularly memorable. My cousin, Weyli, and I would inevitably get bored and start exploring. She was daring and cool and made these never-ending meals exciting. She could make anything feel like an adventure, like riding the elevators up and down until a hotel employee would tell us to stop, or asking our parents for quarters then buying tampons in the ladies' restroom. We had no idea what they were, but when you ran them under water, they'd expand like tea bags! We used to flick them on the ceiling and watch them splatter on the ground. This was hilarious to us, until again, we'd get in trouble. Every half hour or so, we'd run back to the table to see how many courses were left to go, continuing to play until the dessert course arrived. Exhausted from all our fun, we'd quickly fall asleep in the car on the way home.

When Weyli wasn't there and I was the only child at the table, I would go into the kitchen and watch Sao Shan, our pastry chef, knead and roll out dough. She sat in a narrow dry goods closet with a small table and churned out scallion pancakes, dumplings, and red bean pastries. I sat next to her and watched silently until she gave me a piece of dough to play with.

While I loved these outings, I liked being home or at Lau Lau's house even more. On Sundays, we would gather at my grandma's house, where she often served my favorites: Beijing meat sauce and dumplings. I loved to watch my grandmother, my mom, and my aunt make the dumplings together. I was used to seeing them all dressed up for a night out in their beautiful clothing and jewelry, with full makeup, but here, everyone was casual and comfortable, wearing warm-up suits and cooking together. With piles of steaming dumplings in the middle of the table and the whole family seated together, these dinners were loud with big smiles and laughter all around.

My parents would often entertain at home for family and friends. My mom, with the help of our housekeeper, would cook dish after dish. From my perch at the kids' table in the kitchen, I watched as she approached the formal dining room with each course, greeted with applause and celebration that grew louder as the night went on. We could smell the cigarettes as the men drank and smoked. After dessert, the adults would progress into the basement for late night games, and I would fall asleep to the faint sound of mixing mahjong tiles.

WHEN I WAS TEN YEARS OLD, my parents asked me if I wanted to go to upstate New York to train with an Olympic skating coach for the summer. There, I boarded with an older couple, Mr. & Mrs. Jennings, who drove me to skating every day and fed me my meals. I missed home,

On Sundays, we would gather at my grandma's house, where she often served my favorites: Beijing meat sauce and dumplings. I loved to watch my grandmother, my mom, and my aunt make the dumplings together.

but also liked living in an American household. Mrs. Jennings was an excellent cook and made mashed potatoes, chicken pot pie, Swedish meatballs, and German chocolate cake from scratch. The skating was hard work, but I was happy to be exposed to other young, competitive skaters from all over the country. At the end of the summer, I was given the opportunity to stay and train during my fifth-grade school year. I skated and trained more than I was in school—beyond skating, I spent all my time in the gym, doing off-ice skills training and ballet. Instead of my usual buns and noodles, I drank protein shakes after school. That fall, my mom and my sisters moved to upstate New York to be with me. Nicole was two years old, and Christina was nineteen. There, we lived in a tiny two-bedroom apartment, which felt very different from our big fancy house at home. It felt like life was changing fast.

I felt something shift within our family, but it wasn't something we talked about, and I didn't dare to ask. Throughout that year, my dad drove from Boston every other weekend to visit us, taking Nicole and me out each time. I continued to work hard on my skating, and that January, right before my eleventh birthday, I achieved a major dream: I was to perform at Rockefeller Center in New York City. My skating had never been better, but I was starting to realize that I was not the best. For the first time, I felt that my skating was stagnant and that I was hitting a wall. That summer, before sixth grade, my father sat me down. "How many Kristi Yamaguchis are there in this world?" he asked. "Only one," I answered. "How many girls in this world want to be the next Kristi? And what are the chances that you will become the best in the world?" I understood. But then, he told me I had a big decision to make. He said, "In two weeks, I am coming back to New York. You need to decide if you would like to stay in New York and continue to train like this, or if you want to move back to Weston with me, go to school, skate recreationally, and be a normal kid. You and Nicole will live with me, and mom will stay here." That's when I knew that I had to choose between my parents, and from this moment on, I realized that we were not going to be a family like we were before. I decided to go back to Weston with my father and Nicole to be a normal kid. But this felt so scary and different—what would life be like without my mother living at home?

MY TIME WAS NOW SPLIT between Weston during the school year, and with my mom in New Jersey during the summer months. She quickly established a new Sally Ling's restaurant in Fort Lee. I was in awe of my mom's new life and how she was able to create something so successful. Her new home was a quick twenty-minute drive from Manhattan, and she brought us to fancy restaurants like Le Cirque, Daniel Boulud, and Jean Georges. Back in Weston, my dad asked me to help at the Sally Ling's in Newton. I was only twelve years old, but I learned how to pack take-out, and eventually I made my way to working the front of the house. He encouraged me, reasoning that it would help me feel more comfortable around people and relieve some of my shyness. Dad taught me how to stand up straight

NADIA LIU MEASURES INGREDIENTS FOR CHINESE SESAME SAUCE.

and walk around the dining room with a strong posture. He made me rehearse how to answer the phone and talk to customers. He was right: working in the restaurant on Friday and Saturday nights helped me become more confident. In hindsight, this was all part of his plan—to coach me and instill self-esteem. During the summers, I worked at Sally Ling's in New Jersey, and my mom was impressed with my ability to pick up the phones with ease, multitasking in her busy and buzzing restaurant.

I was happy to be back in Weston, going to public school and being with my friends. On the last day of seventh grade, my friends and I were at a diner in the center of town, eating grilled cheese and celebrating the end of the school year. A group of boys walked in and joined us, including a boy I knew from elementary school, Kyle Spellman. I'd always thought he was so cute and cool, and here he was, eating grilled cheese with us and becoming a close friend. We were inseparable for years, and remained best of friends until sophomore year of high school, when he became my boyfriend.

During my high school years, my dad took us on trips all over Italy, Taiwan, and beyond, making the world feel very small. No matter where we went in the world, he always had a local friend to show us around and share the specialties of the region. My dad took us to eat at the cheapest street food vendors and then to the fanciest restaurants so we could understand the full range of food. We analyzed the dining experiences together, calling it "R&D." I loved watching him steal menus from these restaurants; he used these trips to find inspiration for new dishes to serve at the restaurant.

During my senior year of high school, my dad decided to split the Newton Centre Sally Ling's space in half to introduce a new concept, while still satisfying our long-time customers. He noticed how much Nicole loved sushi; he decided it would do well in Newton—and Nicole could have as much sushi as she wanted. He gave me an assignment: write the menu for the new concept. I was to go to the library, check out books on Japan, and collect menus from all the surrounding Japanese restaurants. I had to research and prepare for our regular meetings where he drilled me with questions, critiqued my choices, and suggested unique dishes that would differentiate us from the competition. When we launched Azuma that spring, I felt so proud of my

hard work and my involvement in the process. I realize that my dad did this to give me first-hand experience in creating a concept, setting goals, and going through the hard work to bring those plans to life.

Meanwhile, my mom was running a booming business in New Jersey. On busy weekend nights, they had to staff six delivery drivers. My parents built Sally Ling's together, and after their divorce, they each continued to create new, successful ventures on their own. I admired their strong work ethic and perseverance and was impressed by how hard they worked.

My formative years were spent celebrating family, fine dining, travel, and dedication to an all-consuming sport, but they also involved family separation and emotionally challenging times. Every year brought progress and growth; I clearly remember

Over the years, my dad helped me to think deeply about how life advances and changes shape us, and how we should always be better and smarter than yesterday. My mom was always there to support me and educate me in her own way. She showed me that women can accomplish anything they set their minds to.

feeling each August, as I left New Jersey and returned to Weston, that I was a wholly different person going into the new school year. Over the years, my dad helped me to think deeply about how life advances and changes shape us, and how we should always be better and smarter than yesterday. My mom was always there to support me and educate me in her own way. She showed me that women can accomplish anything they set their minds to. Although they went through a tough divorce, I know they were better parents as a result. I believe by being apart, they were each able to individually live to their full potential. They had to make themselves happy in order to be healthy for us. I am who I am today because of them, and the lessons they taught me along the way. I only hope I can be half as good as them in all that I do.

CHINESE NEW YEAR SWEET RICE CAKE

年糕　**Serves up to 8 people**

I've always loved celebrating Chinese New Year, a date that moves according to the moon's phases. In our family, Chinese New Year meant red envelopes of lucky money for the kids and family meals with cousins, at home and at our restaurants. The New Year meals would consist of dumplings, noodles, spring rolls, and fresh whole fish—dishes we ate year-round, but made more exciting because of the holiday. My mom's sweet, sticky rice cake was always a highlight. It's a steamed cake, cooked on your stovetop. Traditionally, eating "nian gao" for the New Year ensured you'd be promoted in the coming year. I didn't think about promotions as a kid, but I always ate as much as I could—especially for breakfast.

During Chinese New Year, red is the color of good luck, which is why my mother always added a touch of red food coloring to her rice cake. Feel free to do the same or skip that step.

Flower Simple Syrup

1½ cups sugar

1 tablespoon Osmanthus flower syrup

⅛ teaspoon red food coloring (optional)

12 pieces Chinese red dates or Medjool dates

4 cups sweet rice flour

3 large eggs

Vegetable oil, for searing

Prep list

MAKE THE SIMPLE SYRUP: Bring 2 cups of water to a boil over high heat. Add the sugar, turn off the heat, and stir to dissolve. Add the Osmanthus flower syrup and mix well. Set aside to cool, then add red food coloring if using.

CUT THE DATES lengthwise and remove the pits.

Cooking

Put the sweet rice flour in a large mixing bowl. Add the simple syrup and mix with a big spoon until well incorporated and the texture is wet and paste-like.

Place the dough in a 9-inch round cake pan. (My mother prefers to use a disposable tin cake pan because it steams quickly, but a reusable one also works.) Push the dates into the dough, skin-side up so they're flush with the dough's surface.

Prepare a steamer pot. If you do not have a steamer, here's a handy trick: make balls of aluminum foil (about the size of golf balls) and place them in the bottom of the pot. Place a baking dish on top of the aluminum foil balls, ensuring the water does not touch the baking dish. Steam the cake for one hour or until an inserted chopstick comes out clean.

Let the rice cake cool and place overnight in the refrigerator.

Finish and Serve

When ready to eat, slice the rice cake into rectangles, approximately 2 inches long by 1½ inches wide, about ½ inch thick. Whisk the eggs in a bowl, then submerge the pieces of rice cake in the egg.

Heat a non-stick pan over medium heat. Add enough oil to cover the bottom of the pan. When the oil is hot, pan-sear the sweet rice cake until the outside is browned and crispy. Take your time, as you want the rice cake to soften and become tender in the process. Serve immediately, as it's best hot off the pan!

CRYSTAL SHRIMP

清炒虾仁   **Serves 4**

My dad used to say the test of a good chef is their version of crystal shrimp. He would ask every prospective chef to make it, and I understand why: once you try a good version, you can never eat anything less. The simplicity of the dish makes it a challenge to execute perfectly. The shrimp must be fresh and dry, the cooking temperature must be hot but not too hot, and just the right amount of cornstarch must be used. The result is light and crisp, making it a perfect match for bolder, heavier dishes.

1 pound shrimp
  (16-20 per pound)

½ teaspoon cornstarch,
  plus more for slurry

1 tablespoon vegetable oil,
  plus more for cooking

½ teaspoon salt

1 teaspoon sugar

1 tablespoon Shaoxing rice wine

Prep list

PEEL AND DEVEIN THE SHRIMP, then rinse with cold water. Pat shrimp dry with a paper towel.

IN A MEDIUM BOWL, mix the cornstarch with 1 tablespoon vegetable oil. Add the shrimp and toss to coat evenly. Cover and place in the fridge for at least 20 minutes.

MAKE A CORNSTARCH SLURRY. In a small bowl combine 1 tablespoon of cornstarch with 1 tablespoon of water, mixing until smooth. If cornstarch and water separate over time, you may need to mix again before adding.

Cooking

Heat a medium pan over medium heat. Once the pan is hot, add 3 tablespoons of the oil. When it shimmers, add the shrimp and cook until they begin to turn pink, about 2 minutes. Toss or flip the shrimp as needed to ensure both sides are evenly cooked. Add the salt, the sugar, and the wine and continue to cook until the shrimp turns an orangey pink, about 1 minute more. Check to ensure that the shrimp is cooked through.

Slowly add the cornstarch slurry and mix well. Continue cooking until the sauce thickens and the shrimp looks glossy.

DAD'S FAVORITE LION'S HEAD WITH NAPA CABBAGE

紅燒獅子頭 **Yields 10 large meatballs**

I remember sitting in the booth of our Newton Centre location, face to face with my dad, eating Lion's Head. In one hand, he held a bowl of rice topped with a giant meatball, in the other, chopsticks. "This is what you call comfort food!" he exclaimed. I'd never heard the term "comfort food," but I understood what he meant. Whenever I eat these meatballs, whether in soup or with sauce over napa cabbage, it brings me comfort because I think about my dad.

Meatballs

1 pound ground pork

½ cup panko

½ cup chicken broth

½ cup water chestnuts, diced

1 egg

1 scallion, trimmed and chopped

2-inch piece fresh ginger root, peeled and minced

1 teaspoon sugar

1 teaspoon soy sauce

1 teaspoon Shaoxing rice wine

1 teaspoon sesame oil

1 teaspoon salt

⅛ teaspoon white pepper

¼ teaspoon five spice powder

3 cups plus 3 tablespoons vegetable oil, divided

2-inch piece fresh ginger root, peeled and cut into thin medallions

½ head napa cabbage (about 1 pound), chopped into 3-inch pieces

½ teaspoon sea salt

1 cup chicken broth

Prep list

MAKE THE MEATBALL MIXTURE: In a large bowl, combine the meatball ingredients and mix well to tenderize the meat. (My mom insists you stir for 5 to 6 minutes.)

LINE A BAKING SHEET with paper towels for the finished meatballs.

PREPARE AND MEASURE the remaining ingredients.

Cooking

Heat 3 cups of the vegetable oil to 250°F in a medium sauce pot over medium heat. (A pot about 6 to 8 inches in diameter works best; you will require less oil and limit the mess.)

Form the meatball mixture into 2-inch balls and carefully place in the oil. Fry the meatballs, turning as needed, until firm and cooked through, about 7 to 10 minutes. Remove with a slotted metal spoon and transfer to the prepared baking sheet to absorb the excess oil. Fry in batches of 3 to 4 meatballs. Set aside.

Heat a large pan over medium heat. Once the pan is hot, add 3 tablespoons of the vegetable oil. When it shimmers, add the ginger and toast until golden, about 1 minute.

Reduce the heat to medium-low, add the cabbage and the salt, and cook for about 2 minutes.

Add the chicken broth and the meatballs, cover and simmer for about 6 minutes or until the cabbage is tender, making sure that the broth doesn't fully evaporate. Remove the ginger and discard.

To serve, place the napa cabbage in a bowl or serving platter, top with the meatballs, and pour the residual sauce over them.

SALLY LING'S IMPERIAL CHICKEN

湘鸡 **Serves 4**

One of my earliest memories is of orange peels on the kitchen windowsill. Once they were dry and hard, my mom would bring them to the restaurant to make this dish. Sally Ling's Imperial Chicken was by far one of the most popular dishes on her menu. Especially with my little sister Nicole, who could eat it five nights in a row. Similar to General Tso's Chicken, the crispy chicken is coated with a sweet and spicy orange sauce. We used to serve it piled high and surrounded by steamed broccoli florets.

1 pound chicken thighs,
  trimmed of fat and cut
  into 2-inch cubes

Marinade

2 cloves garlic, peeled
  and minced

1-inch piece fresh ginger root,
  peeled and minced

1 tablespoon fish sauce

1 tablespoon cooking wine

½ teaspoon sea salt

½ teaspoon five spice powder

Sauce

1 clove garlic, peeled
  and minced

2 tablespoons orange juice

2 tablespoons rice vinegar

1 tablespoon soy sauce

2 teaspoons orange liqueur,
  such as Cointreau or
  Grand Marnier

½-inch piece fresh ginger root,
  peeled and minced

½ cup brown sugar

½ cup cornstarch, plus
  more for slurry

3 cups vegetable oil, for frying

¼ cup dried orange peel

Prep list

MAKE THE MARINADE: In a small bowl, combine the marinade ingredients and the chicken and toss; marinate for at least 1 hour in the refrigerator.

MAKE THE SAUCE: In a small bowl, combine the sauce ingredients and mix well.

LINE A BAKING SHEET with paper towels for the finished chicken.

MAKE A CORNSTARCH SLURRY: In a small bowl, combine 2 tablespoons of cornstarch with 2 tablespoons of water, mixing until smooth. If the cornstarch and water separate over time, you may need to mix again before using.

PREPARE AND MEASURE the remaining ingredients.

Cooking

When ready to fry, dredge the marinated chicken with cornstarch. Make sure the chicken is fully coated and shake off any excess.

Heat the oil to 375°F in a medium sauce pot over medium heat. (A pot about 6 to 8 inches in diameter works best; you will require less oil and limit the mess.)

Using a slotted metal spoon, gently place the chicken in the oil. Fry in small batches until the chicken is cooked through, about 3 minutes. Check for doneness by cutting the thickest piece of chicken in half. Transfer to the prepared baking sheet to absorb the excess oil.

Heat a large pan over medium heat. Add the sauce. Cook for about 2 minutes or until the sugar has dissolved, stirring constantly to avoid burning it.

Increase the heat to high and add the chicken and the orange peels. Toss the chicken in the sauce, making sure to coat it evenly. Cook for about 1 minute more.

Give the cornstarch slurry a good mix and drizzle it into the sauce, mixing continuously until the sauce has thickened and the chicken is covered and glossy. Serve with greens for color!

SUNDAY CONGEE

白粥 **Serves 2**

The best part about going to college close to home? Sundays with my dad and sister. From brunch to dinner time, I spent every Sunday with my dad and Nicole, doing laundry while Boston's classical station, WCRB, played in the living room.

Our regular breakfast menu ranged from waffles and pancakes to noodle soups with leftovers. But more often than not, Sunday brunch featured Chinese congee: my dad would prepare it alongside tofu, thousand-year eggs, fresh herbs, and a soy and sesame oil dressing. He served it with a giant soup spoon, and it would magically disappear by the end of the meal. A recipe for my favorite way to eat congee can be found below—and though the thousand-year eggs may be an acquired taste, I had to include them. My dad used to say, "If anyone likes smelly French blue cheese, they will like thousand-year eggs!"

Congee

½ cup medium grain white rice (look for US #1)

½ teaspoon salt

MY FAVORITE CONGEE

2 thousand-year eggs, store-bought, or 2 Marble Tea Eggs, pg. 48

1 scallion, trimmed and finely chopped

5 sprigs cilantro (stems included), finely chopped

1 block silken soft tofu

2 tablespoons soy sauce

1 teaspoon sesame oil

Prep list

RINSE AND DRAIN THE RICE 3 times in cold water to ensure the rice is fully cleaned. Soak the rice in 2 cups of water overnight or for at least 12 hours.

STRAIN THE RICE and discard the water.

Cooking

Add the rice and 7 cups of water to a large heavy-bottomed pot. Bring to a boil over high heat.

Once boiling, reduce the heat to medium-low and cover with a lid. Stir occasionally to prevent the rice from sticking to the bottom or clumping together. The rice will expand and melt into the water to create a rice porridge.

Simmer until the congee is thick and creamy, about 1 to 1½ hours. The congee will thicken even after you remove it from the heat. Add the salt and enjoy with your favorite side dishes and toppings.

Here's how we do it: peel and slice each egg lengthwise into 6 wedges. Rinse the tofu and slice into ½-inch cubes. It's okay if the tofu is not perfect—the messiness is the beauty in this dish!

Portion the congee in serving bowls. Plate tofu cubes, egg wedges, a drizzle of the soy sauce and the sesame oil, and garnish with the scallions and the cilantro. In our house, we love pork sung and bamboo in chili oil. Don't forget the giant spoon!

MINCED CHICKEN WITH LETTUCE LEAVES

清炒鸡鬆 **Serves 4**

As a child, I remember how tuxedoed waiters served this dish to customers by French cart, finishing the dish tableside, then serving minced chicken inside bowl-shaped lettuce leaves. The art of the dish is the knife skill required. This preparation is refined, clean, and classic—as elegant as the dining room at Sally Ling's on the waterfront. It remains popular at Dumpling Daughter today.

½ pound boneless, skinless chicken breast

1¼ teaspoon salt, divided

1 teaspoon cornstarch

3½ tablespoons vegetable oil, divided

2 medium dry shiitake mushrooms, soaked in warm water for 25 minutes

2 stalks celery

2 small carrots

1 tablespoons Shaoxing rice wine

¼ teaspoon white pepper

Hoisin sauce

8 large Bibb or butter lettuce leaves

Prep list

MINCE THE CHICKEN into small ¼-inch pieces, similar in size to corn kernels. Combine 1 teaspoon of the salt, the cornstarch, and 1½ tablespoons of the oil in a medium bowl. Add the chicken and stir to mix. Chill for at least 30 minutes in the refrigerator.

ONCE SOAKED, REMOVE THE MUSHROOMS from the water. Cut off and discard the stems. Mince the mushrooms into pieces the same size as the chicken.

PEEL OFF THE OUTERMOST LAYER of the celery to remove the tough, stringy pieces. Slice the celery lengthwise into ¼-inch thick matchsticks. Rotate and mince the celery into pieces the same size as the chicken.

PEEL, CHOP, AND MINCE the carrots in the same manner.

Cooking

Heat a large pan over medium heat. Once the pan is hot, add 1 tablespoon of the oil. When it shimmers, add the chicken and cook until just turned white, about 2 minutes. Remove from the pan and set aside.

Return the same pan to high heat and add the remaining oil. When it is hot, add the celery, the carrots, and the mushrooms and cook, stirring continuously, until tender, about 2 minutes. Add the chicken, the wine, the remaining salt, and the white pepper and mix well to incorporate.

To serve, spoon the hoisin sauce onto a lettuce leaf, then place a mound of minced chicken on top. I like to serve the lettuce leaf cups to my guests and have them build their own at the table.

CLASSIC NAPA CABBAGE WITH DRIED SHRIMP

开陽白菜 **Serves 4 as a side**

This was a staple in our house for as long as I can remember. Light and flavorful, it's one of those vegetable dishes that rounds out any meal. Traditionally, it is enjoyed alongside other dishes, but I have friends who love it so much they'd eat a bowl for dinner. Dried shrimp is a beautiful and tasty ingredient that makes the dish extra delicious. It keeps in the fridge for months, making it an easy savory addition to many meals. You may have to make a run to your local Chinese market, but I urge you to try it. See Stocking a Chinese Pantry (pg. 18) for tips.

½ head napa cabbage, about 1 pound

2 tablespoons dried shrimp

2 teaspoons cornstarch

2 tablespoons vegetable oil

½ cup chicken broth

½ teaspoon salt

Prep list

ROUGHLY CHOP the firm stem of the cabbage into pieces about 3 inches by 1½ inches in size. The leaves can be chopped slightly larger.

PUT THE SHRIMP in a microwave safe bowl, submerge with water, and microwave on high for 1 minute. Drain water.

MAKE A CORNSTARCH SLURRY: In a small bowl, combine 2 teaspoons of cornstarch with 2 tablespoons of water, mixing until smooth. If the cornstarch and water separate over time, you may need to mix again before using.

Cooking

Heat a large pan over medium heat. Once the pan is hot, add the oil. When it shimmers, add the shrimp and the napa cabbage and cook until slightly softened, about 30 seconds.

Add the chicken broth and the salt and mix. Cover and cook until the cabbage is tender, about 3 minutes. Add salt to taste.

Turn the heat to high, add the cornstarch slurry, mix well, and cook until sauce thickens.

LOBSTER
TWO WAYS

WHEN LONGTIME CUSTOMERS OF SALLY LING'S talk about their favorite dish, it usually involves lobster. A word of warning: this recipe is not for every home cook. It's challenging to cut the live lobster if you've never done it before. However, the result is most definitely rewarding and delicious. You will not find stir-fried lobster in many places, as lobster is not authentic in Chinese cuisine—they don't swim in the local waters! This was purely a creative way that my parents embraced the best ingredients around, which is indeed New England lobster.

How to Take Apart a Live Lobster

This process will require a heavy cleaver, an apron or a disposable shirt, and a good cutting board. Cutting a lobster is not easy, but very rewarding when complete. To cut the lobster into pieces, first place the victim in the freezer for 15 minutes so it doesn't move while you cut it. If you feel guilty putting the lobster in the freezer, then you'll have to kill it while it's moving.

Pierce the head with the corner of a cleaver, about 2 inches below the eyes, pushing straight down in the middle of the head. Remove the shell of the head and set aside. Twist and remove the front legs and claws from the body. Twist and separate the knuckles (the two joints connecting the claws to the body) from the claws. Crack the knuckles with the broadside of the cleaver to make them easier to open once served. Crack each claw in half lengthwise with the back of the cleaver and cut at the crack to cleanly separate the claw into two pieces. Remove the small walking legs from the bodies. Remove and discard the lobster gills, tomalley (the green mustard substance found in the body), and innards. Split the tail in half vertically, then cut each half of the tail horizontally twice to create 6 tail pieces. (See the photo diagram opposite.)

SALLY LING'S LOBSTER WITH GINGER & SCALLIONS

薑葱炒龍蝦 **Serves 4 as part of a family meal**

2 lobsters, 1½ pounds each

Sauce

¼ cup Shaoxing rice wine

1 tablespoon sugar

2 tablespoons soy sauce

½ cup vegetable oil

3-inch piece fresh ginger root, peeled and thinly sliced

6 scallions, trimmed and cut into 3-inch long pieces

Prep list

MAKE THE SAUCE: In a small bowl, combine the sauce ingredients and mix.

CUT LOBSTER according to directions, pg. 72.

PREPARE AND MEASURE the remaining ingredients.

Cooking

Heat a large pan over medium-high heat. Once the pan is hot, add the oil. When it shimmers, add all the lobster pieces (including the head) and cook for about 5 minutes, turning pieces continuously so they cook evenly. The head will be the first part to finish cooking, as there is not much meat in it; once the head is red all over, remove and set aside on a serving platter.

Add the ginger and cook until all the lobster pieces turn a red-orange color, about 4 minutes more. Add the scallions and the sauce and cook until all the pieces of lobster meat are white, about 2 minutes more. Arrange on a platter and serve.

LOBSTER CANTONESE STYLE

廣式龍蝦 **Serves 4 as part of a family meal**

2 lobsters, 1½ pounds each

Sauce

3 tablespoons Shaoxing
rice wine

2 tablespoons soy sauce

1 teaspoon sugar

½ cup water

1 small yellow onion, peeled
and diced

4 ounces ground pork,
about ½ cup

2 tablespoons dòuchǐ
(fermented black beans),
soaked overnight and
rinsed thoroughly

4 cloves garlic, peeled and
finely chopped

2-inch piece fresh ginger root,
peeled and finely chopped

2 eggs

2 scallions, trimmed and
finely chopped

½ cup vegetable oil

Prep list

MAKE THE SAUCE: In a small bowl, combine the sauce ingredients and mix.

IN ANOTHER SMALL BOWL, combine the onion and the ground pork.

DRAIN AND DISCARD the liquid from the black beans, then chop the beans to a size similar to the garlic and the ginger. In a third small bowl, combine the fermented black beans, the garlic, and the ginger.

IN A FOURTH SMALL BOWL, crack the eggs, add the scallions, and whisk well.

CUT LOBSTER according to directions, pg. 72.

Cooking

Heat a large pan over medium heat. Once the pan is hot, add the oil. When it shimmers, add the ground pork and onion mixture. Cook, separating the pork into small bits, until the pork begins to brown, about 2 minutes.

Increase the heat to high, add the lobster and the black bean mixture, and stir-fry for about 3 minutes.

Reduce the heat to medium, add the sauce, cover with a lid, and cook until the lobster is red and fully cooked, about 3 to 5 minutes.

Uncover and mix, coating the lobster evenly with the sauce.

Increase the heat to high again, add the scallion and egg mixture, and stir until the eggs are cooked, about 1 minute.

There will be residual oil. Using a slotted spoon, carefully remove the lobster pieces and the pork and bean mixture, leaving any excess oil in the pan. Arrange on a platter, top with the pork and bean mixture, and serve.

GRANDPA'S RED-COOKED PIGS FEET

红燒豬手 **Serves 4**

My grandfather, who I called Lau Yea (姥爷) meaning "my mother's father," loved this dish. Lau Yea took a lot of pride in making it just right every time. He was not a cook by any means, but he knew how to make delicious pigs feet. The tasty, slippery, and tender skin is unlike anything else and is best served with white rice. Sadly, I never asked Lau Yea for his recipe, so my mom worked on this version to best capture his flavors. A tip: ask your butcher to cut the pigs feet into small pieces per the instructions, as you won't be able to cut them with a normal knife at home. This dish is not for everyone—only the most gourmet!

2 pounds pig feet

Braise

3 tablespoons cooking wine

2 cups chicken broth

3 tablespoons soy sauce

2 teaspoons salt

3 pieces whole star anise

2 tablespoons vegetable oil

3-inch piece fresh ginger root, peeled and smashed with the flat of a knife

¼ cup rock candy

½ cup chicken broth, optional

Prep list

MAKE THE BRAISING LIQUID: In a large bowl, add the cooking wine, the broth, the soy sauce, the salt, and the star anise.

PREPARE AND MEASURE the remaining ingredients.

Cooking

Bring 8 cups of water to a boil over high heat. Add the pigs feet. Cook until the water returns to a boil, then strain the pigs feet and rinse with cold water. (This will remove any impurities from the protein and ensure the best flavor.)

Heat a Dutch oven over medium heat. Once it's hot, add the oil. When it shimmers, add the fresh ginger and the pigs feet and cook until the ginger is golden, about 2 minutes. Add the braising liquid and bring to a boil, then reduce the heat to the lowest setting. Cover and simmer for 2 hours, stirring every 30 minutes or so.

At the 2-hour mark, the meat should be tender; check by poking it with a chopstick or fork. Increase the heat to high and add the rock sugar, mixing until it melts. If there isn't enough liquid, add the chicken broth. The finished sauce should be thick and sticky.

Plate the pigs feet on a platter, pour the sauce over the top, and serve. The sauce is amazing over a simple bowl of white rice.

SALLY LING'S VEGETABLE SPRING ROLLS

素菜春卷 **Yields 12 Spring Rolls**

Spring rolls were a classic appetizer at Sally Ling's, and they're so delicious I had to put them on the Dumpling Daughter menu too. At the restaurant, we freshly roll them every day. When I make them at home, I fry them earlier in the day and then reheat them in the oven for 10 minutes at 350°F when my guests arrive. Perfection! You can never have just one. They've been a best seller for decades for a reason.

Filling

3 dried shiitake mushrooms, soaked in warm water for 25 minutes

½ head flat or green cabbage (about 1 pound), thinly shredded into 2-inch strips

3 small carrots, peeled and julienned to 2-inches long

2 scallions, trimmed, halved lengthwise, and chopped into 2-inch pieces

3 tablespoons vegetable oil

1 teaspoon sugar

1 teaspoon salt

¼ teaspoon white pepper

12 spring roll skins, store-bought (plus extra, in case some rip)

1 egg, or 1 tablespoon all-purpose flour (to "glue" the rolls)

3 cups vegetable oil, for frying

Prep list

REMOVE THE MUSHROOMS from the water. Cut off and discard the stems, then thinly slice the mushrooms.

LINE A BAKING SHEET with paper towels for the finished spring rolls.

PREPARE AND MEASURE the remaining ingredients.

Cooking

Make the filling: Heat a large pan over medium heat. Once the pan is hot, add the 3 tablespoons of oil. When it shimmers, add the cabbage, the carrots, and the mushrooms and cook, stirring frequently, until all the vegetables are tender, about 10 minutes.

Add the scallions, the sugar, the salt, and the white pepper. Mix to combine. Let cool at room temperature. You can spread the filling on a baking sheet to speed the cooling process.

Before you begin wrapping, make the "glue," either by whisking the egg or by combining the flour and 1 tablespoon of warm water. Set aside.

When the filling has cooled, wrap the spring rolls (see photo instructions on next page): Place the spring roll skin at a 45-degree angle, with the corner pointing at you. Place ¼ cup of the filling on the skin. Tightly roll the skin over and fold in the sides to trap the filling. Continue rolling, keeping the filling loose but being firm with the rolling. Paint the edges of the skin with the glue.

Fry the spring rolls: Over medium heat, bring the 3 cups of oil to 350°F in a medium sauce pot. (A pot about 6 to 8 inches in diameter works best; you will require less oil and limit the mess.)

Gently place the spring rolls into the oil to prevent splatter. Fry until golden, about 90 seconds, turning the spring rolls halfway through.

Remove with a slotted metal spoon or tongs, and transfer to the prepared baking sheet to absorb the excess oil.

SIMPLE SPARERIB & DAIKON SOUP

排骨蘿蔔湯 **Serves 4 as an appetizer**

This classic Chinese homestyle soup is my favorite thing to make in the winter, filling my home with warmth and comfort. The trick to this rich soup is to make it the night before—the flavors will improve with time, and you can easily skim the fat off the top before reheating.

1½ to 2 pounds pork rib tips, bone-in (pork rib, tip, and end cuts are fine to use as long as there's meat and bones)

1 medium daikon (about 1 pound), peeled

2-inch piece fresh ginger root, peeled and roughly chopped into ½-inch pieces

1 tablespoon salt, or to taste

2 scallions (greens only), trimmed and chopped into ¼-inch pieces

---

Prep list

TRIM THE FAT from the spareribs, then slice them into 2-inch pieces each with 1 to 2 bones.

CUT THE DAIKON, using an oblique cut, into 1½-inch pieces.

PREPARE AND MEASURE the remaining ingredients.

Cooking

Place the pork in a large stock pot and cover with water. Over high heat, bring the pot to a boil. When grayish foam rises to the top, remove from heat and pour out water. (This will remove any impurities from the protein and ensure the best flavor.) Rinse the pork and wash the pot, then return the pork to the clean pot.

Submerge the pork again, making sure to cover with 1 inch of cold water. Add the ginger, cover the pot, and bring to a boil over high heat. Once boiling, partially uncover the pot, reduce the heat to medium, and simmer for 30 minutes.

Add the daikon and simmer until it is fork tender, about 15 minutes. Add the salt to taste. It is always better to start off under-seasoning. Refrigerate, overnight if possible.

When ready to serve, skim excess fat off the top for the cleanest broth and reheat. Portion and garnish with the scallions. Include an empty bowl on the table for discarding the bones. We love having a dish of soy sauce to dip the ribs in!

HANDMADE WONTONS

猪肉云吞 **Yields 24 Wontons**

Not sure what a wonton is? I describe it as a Chinese tortellini. I also describe them as delicate bites of heaven. Wontons can be enjoyed in many ways—I love them in soup, but also dressed with sesame sauce and red chili oil and garnished with cilantro and chopped scallions. Make a lot and freeze for later use. The wontons in my freezer are like the blue jeans in my closet: they are reliable and go with everything!

Wonton Filling

½ pound ground pork, chicken, or turkey

1 scallion, trimmed and chopped

½-inch piece fresh ginger root, peeled and minced

1 teaspoon light soy sauce

½ teaspoon salt

¼ teaspoon sugar

1 teaspoon sesame oil

Dash white pepper

24 wonton wrappers, store-bought (plus extra, in case some rip)

Prep list

MAKE THE WONTON FILLING: In a bowl, combine the ingredients and mix thoroughly.

LINE A BAKING SHEET with parchment paper for the finished wontons.

Wrapping Wontons

Using a spoon or chopsticks, place ½ teaspoon of the wonton filling in the center of each skin. This is very important: don't overstuff your wonton or it will be more difficult to wrap and won't cook fully. Paint water around the edge of the wrapper and fold it in half to create a rectangle, making sure to create a tight seal with the wetted edges and with no trapped air. Roll the top half of the wrapper back over itself. Bring the two corners of the folded edge together and pinch tightly to seal.

Arrange the wontons on the prepared baking sheet as you work.

If saving for later, place the tray of wontons in the freezer. When the wontons are completely frozen, transfer them to a plastic bag. They are perfectly fine for up to 4 months.

Cooking Wontons

Bring 6 cups of water to a boil over high heat. Carefully place 12 to 18 wontons into the boiling water with a slotted spoon. Immediately stir to prevent them from sticking to the bottom and sides. Boil wontons over high heat for about 3 minutes, gently stirring occasionally. (Frozen wontons may take a minute longer.) Once the wontons float, cook for another minute or so. Take one out to test it! The internal temperature should be 165°F, and the filling should be cooked through.

Use wontons in Sally Ling's Wonton Soup (pg. 85), Sesame Wontons (pg. 174), or simply drizzle with Perfect Dumpling Sauce (pg. 41) and enjoy!

SALLY LING'S WONTON SOUP

云吞湯　**Serves 4**

In 1984, an order of wonton soup was $1.75 at Sally Ling's. It was my absolute favorite thing to eat growing up. I would go into the restaurant kitchen, ladle the fresh chicken broth out myself, and ask the chef to steep a few wontons for me. Today, we include this dish on the Dumpling Daughter menu for $7—oh, how times have changed. To this day, I find comfort when enjoying this dish, and hope you can too.

24 Handmade Wontons, pg. 82

5 cups From Scratch Chicken Broth, pg. 39

2 scallions, trimmed and chopped into ¼-inch pieces

Bring 6 cups of water to a rolling boil over high heat. Carefully place the wontons into the boiling water with a slotted spoon. Immediately stir to prevent them from sticking to the bottom and sides. Boil wontons on high for about 3 minutes, gently stirring occasionally. (Frozen wontons may take a minute longer.) Once the wontons float, cook for another minute or so. Take one out to test it! The internal temperature should be 165°F, and the filling should be cooked through.

Remove the wontons from the water with a slotted spoon and place 6 wontons into each serving bowl.

Heat the chicken broth for about 8 to 10 minutes to desired temperature, approximately 180°F. Ladle the broth into the serving bowls with the wontons. Garnish with the scallions and enjoy!

HOMEMADE DUMPLINGS

OUR RESTAURANT IS CALLED DUMPLING DAUGHTER FOR A REASON. I love dumplings. There is nothing like a homemade version. From our cooking classes and talking with our customers, we know that so many of you want to try making your own dumplings. We applaud this enthusiasm.

A word to the wise: making dumplings at home is not easy and it is not quick. It is one of those life techniques that benefits from a lot of practice. At first, your dumplings may be doughy, too thick, and uneven. Soon, you'll develop experience at making every dumpling skin the same size, thickness, and shape. I still do not make dumpling skins like my mom because she has had more practice than I have!

When you make dumplings at home, you are committing to making a big batch. We wrote these recipes to yield sixty dumplings. In our opinion, if you're going through the trouble to make these, getting your hands and counter dirty, you might as well make extra to freeze! My mom, aunt, and grandma used to sit around the kitchen table and make four times this recipe in order to have plenty of fresh dumplings and extra for the freezer. So, grab some friends or family, learn a new skill together, and have some fun! The result will be delicious and rewarding.

MOM'S DUMPLING DOUGH

餃子麵 **Yields enough dough for approximately 60 dumplings**

So you want to make your dumplings from scratch—good for you! But first, a lesson on the importance of water temperature. When our pastry chef at Sally Ling's makes scallion pancakes, dumplings, or noodles, she always emphasizes how important the temperature of the water is, and she's the real expert on these matters!

    For boiled dumplings, you will want to use cold water. Cold water produces a dough that is a bit firmer, whereas warm water makes a softer dough.

    If you are making dough for pan-seared dumplings, use warm water (defined as ½ boiling water and ½ room temperature water.) If you're undecided how the dumplings will be prepared, or if you're doing a combination of styles, use warm water.

4 cups all-purpose flour, plus more for kneading the dough

½ teaspoon salt

1⅓ cup water (see headnote about water temperature)

Mixing Dough

Combine the flour and the salt in a large mixing bowl. Add half the water while mixing with a pair of chopsticks. Little by little, add more water and continue to mix. The dough will look flaky at first—be patient.

You can also use a stand mixer with a dough hook attachment. Place the flour and the salt in the bowl. Slowly add the water, pouring in a steady stream while mixing on low speed. Mix until the dough comes together, approximately 3 minutes on the lowest speed.

You don't have to use all the water—just enough to make the dough smooth. The dough should be moist, but not sticking to your fingers. If it's too wet, you can add more flour, 1 tablespoon at a time.

When the dough comes together, turn it out onto a lightly floured surface so you can work with more freedom. Knead the dough with your hands until it becomes smooth. This usually takes about 3 to 5 minutes.

When the dough is smooth and bounces back when you poke it, return it to the mixing bowl and cover it with a wet paper towel. Let it rest for at least one hour. Leave the dough in the refrigerator until ready to wrap the dumplings.

You can let the dough rest overnight, tightly wrapped with plastic wrap in the refrigerator, but make sure to let it come to room temperature 1 hour before you roll it out.

Rolling Out Dumpling Skins

When ready to make the dumplings, turn the dough out onto a lightly floured surface. Cut the ball of dough in half. (First timers may want to quarter their dough, to work with smaller quantities. Keep the remaining portions under a wet paper towel as you roll out the skins and stuff the dumplings, moving on to the remainder as needed, so your dough does not dry out.)

Roll out each portion to create a long rope, about 1 inch in diameter and about 30 inches long. (The rope will be shorter if you're working with smaller batches.) Make sure the rope is cylindrical and the thickness is consistent from end to end—this is important because you want each dough skin to be the same size.

Cut the rope into 1-inch pieces. Place each piece with the cut side down on a lightly floured surface and, with the palm of your hand, press each piece into a circle about the size of a half-dollar coin.

Using a small rolling pin, roll each coin into a wrapper about 3 inches in diameter. Use your dominant hand to roll the pin and use your non-dominant hand to hold the skin. Roll the pin with your palm, starting from the edge of the skin closest to you and rolling no further than the center of the skin. Rotate the skin with your non-dominant hand so the outer perimeter continues to get flattened but the center of the skin stays a bit thicker. (It's important to have the center be thicker because when you wrap the dumplings, the outer edges will come together to seal the dumpling, doubling the thickness.)

It takes time and coordination to get in the rhythm of rolling and turning the dough. This is a skill that can be learned and honed; take your time at the beginning to ensure consistency. (See pg. 91 for technique.)

Wrapping Dumplings

Place about 1 teaspoon of the filling in the center of each dumpling skin (see following recipes for filling ideas). Fold the skin in half over the filling, creating a half moon shape. Tightly pinch and seal the edges that come together, making sure not to trap air inside the dumpling. (See pg. 92 for technique.)

Ensure that the skin is tightly sealed on all sides, or the filling may escape while cooking.

Do your best to work quickly or in small batches, placing the finished dumplings on a prepared baking sheet and moving to the freezer as needed. You don't want the dumplings to sit out at room temperature for more than 1 hour.

If saving for later, place the tray of dumplings in the freezer. When the dumplings are completely frozen, transfer them to a plastic bag and label with the filling name.

MIXING DOUGH

WRAPPING DUMPLINGS

PORK & CABBAGE DUMPLINGS

豬肉白菜饺 **Yields approximately 50 to 60 pieces | Serves 5 for a meal**

Pork and cabbage dumplings have been the most popular dumplings in the United States for over fifty years. Menus across the country offered this dish—sometimes called Peking Ravioli—as an appetizer throughout the 1970s. It was on my parents' menu at Sally Ling's, and I could eat six in one sitting. They were pan-seared and served with ginger soy dipping sauce. Fast forward to today; little has changed. The same delicious recipe is a top seller at Dumpling Daughter—we sell over twenty thousand orders per year!

We recommend pan-searing these dumplings, so if you are making your own dough, use the warm water method.

Filling

4 to 5 large napa cabbage leaves, finely chopped with excess water squeezed out (approximately 2 cups)

2 scallions, trimmed and finely chopped

1 teaspoon fresh ginger root (about ½-inch piece), peeled and finely minced

3 to 4 dried shiitake mushrooms, soaked in warm water for 30 minutes

1 pound ground pork, 80% lean

1 tablespoon sesame oil

1 tablespoon oyster sauce

1 teaspoon soy sauce

½ teaspoon sugar

½ teaspoon sea salt

50 to 60 dumpling skins, pg. 88

4 tablespoons vegetable oil, for cooking

Prep list

REMOVE THE SHIITAKE MUSHROOMS from the water and dry as thoroughly as possible. Cut off and discard the stems, then mince the mushrooms.

MAKE THE FILLING: In a large bowl, combine the filling ingredients and mix. Using chopsticks, stir in a circular motion in one direction for at least 7 to 8 minutes to loosen, break down, and tenderize the meat. Cover the bowl with plastic wrap and leave in the refrigerator until ready to wrap the dumplings.

LINE A BAKING SHEET with parchment paper for the fresh dumplings.

WRAP THE DUMPLINGS according to the directions on pg. 89.

Cooking Method: Pan-Seared

Heat a large pan over high heat. Once the pan is hot, add the 4 tablespoons of vegetable oil. When it shimmers, place the dumplings in concentric circles in the pan, flat side down.

Add enough cold water to the skillet that it comes ½ inch up the side of the dumplings. Cover the pan with a tight-fitting lid and cook over high heat. After about 8 minutes, check on the dumplings. If most of the water has evaporated, uncover and allow the dumplings to absorb any remaining water. With the absence of water, the dumplings will begin to sear. Let the dumplings sizzle until they are golden brown on the bottom.

Carefully remove each dumpling with tongs or a spatula and plate crispy side up. (If they are sticking to the bottom, they aren't done yet; the dumplings will release when they are ready.) If there is excess oil, dab dumplings with a clean paper towel. Cook the remaining dumplings in the same fashion.

Serve alongside our Perfect Dumpling Sauce (pg. 41).

PORK & CHIVE DUMPLINGS

韭菜豬肉餃　**Yields approximately 50 to 60 pieces | Serves 5 for a meal**

These dumplings bring me right back to Grandma's house. Grandma was from Harbin, China and made dumplings in true northern Chinese style, with thicker, chewier skins. The aromatic chives would fill the house with an enticing scent that got us excited for dinner.

　　I like to eat these boiled. (They are also delicious pan-seared, but I like to stick with my family's tradition here!) If you are making the dumpling dough, go with the cold water method.

　　Here's a tip: Cut the chives right before you're ready to wrap the dumplings, then gently mix them into the filling. Wrap right away to envelop the delicious aromas.

Filling

2 large napa cabbage leaves, finely chopped with excess water squeezed out (approximately 1 cup)

1½ teaspoons fresh ginger root (about ½-inch piece), peeled and minced

1 pound ground pork, 80% lean

½ teaspoon salt

½ teaspoon sugar

1 teaspoon soy sauce

1 tablespoon oyster sauce

1 tablespoon sesame oil

3 ounces Chinese chives, chopped (approximately 1½ cups)

50 to 60 dumpling skins, pg. 88

4 tablespoons vegetable oil, for cooking

Prep list

MAKE THE FILLING: In a large bowl, combine the filling ingredients and mix. Using chopsticks, stir in a circular motion in one direction for at least 7 to 8 minutes to loosen, break down, and tenderize the meat. Cover the bowl with plastic wrap and leave in the refrigerator until ready to wrap the dumplings.

LINE A BAKING SHEET with parchment paper for the fresh dumplings.

RIGHT BEFORE you're ready to wrap the dumplings, rinse and dry the chives as thoroughly as possible. Chop them into ¼-inch pieces, and gently fold into the filling.

WRAP THE DUMPLINGS according to the directions on pg. 89.

Cooking Method: Boiling

Bring 6 cups of water to a rapid boil over high heat. Carefully drop in 8 to 12 dumplings at a time and stir immediately to prevent them from sticking to the bottom of the pot. Return to a boil.

Once boiling, add 2 cups of cold water and return to a boil. Once at a rapid boil, reduce heat to medium and continue cooking for about 6 minutes more. The dumplings' internal temperature should reach 165°F. Cut one in half to check for doneness.

Remove the dumplings with a slotted spoon, taking care to shake off any excess water, then place on a serving plate. Cook the remaining dumplings in the same fashion.

Serve alongside our Perfect Dumpling Sauce (pg. 41).

CHICKEN & CABBAGE DUMPLINGS

鸡肉餃子   **Yields approximately 50 to 60 pieces | Serves 5 for a meal**

These were designed for the Dumpling Daughter menu, and good thing we did because kids LOVE them. These dumplings are great boiled or pan-seared, so choose your own adventure; we've given you options for both. If you're making your own dough, use hot or cold water accordingly.

Filling

- 4 to 5 large napa cabbage leaves, finely chopped with excess water squeezed out and thoroughly dried (approximately 2 cups)

- 1 tablespoon fresh ginger root (about ½-inch piece), peeled and finely minced

- 1 pound ground chicken (try to buy thigh or dark meat for most flavor; substitute with ground turkey or white meat chicken if necessary)

- 1½ tablespoons soy sauce

- ½ teaspoon sugar

- ½ teaspoon sea salt

- 2 dashes white pepper

- 50 to 60 dumpling skins, pg. 88

- 4 tablespoons vegetable oil, for cooking

Prep list

MAKE THE FILLING: In a large bowl, combine the filling ingredients and mix. Using chopsticks, stir in a circular motion in one direction for at least 7 to 8 minutes to loosen, break down, and tenderize the meat. Cover the bowl with plastic wrap and leave in the refrigerator until ready to wrap the dumplings.

LINE A BAKING SHEET with parchment paper for the fresh dumplings.

WRAP THE DUMPLINGS according to the directions on pg. 89.

Cooking Method

For this recipe, you can either boil (pg. 94) or pan-sear the dumplings (pg. 93).

Serve alongside our Perfect Dumpling Sauce (pg. 41).

TASTING THE WORLD

Learning Life's Lessons, One Meal at a Time

Rice Cakes Shanghai Style

Ants Climbing on a Tree

Beef with Asparagus

Chicken with Mushrooms in Oyster Sauce

Cold Noodles with Sesame Sauce

Firm Tofu with Chinese Chives & Vegetables

Grand Marnier Shrimp

Homestyle Eggs with Tomatoes

Chinese Chives with Eggs

Kung Pao Chicken

Shredded Lamb with Scallions

Ma-Po Spicy Tofu

Sacha Beef with Tomatoes

Sally Ling's Fried Rice

Shrimp Shanghainese Style

Jumbo Shrimp with Black Bean Sauce

Home Fried Chicken

Hot Pot

MY DAD ALWAYS WANTED ME to go to Wellesley College. Strong, capable women went to Wellesley, it was globally renowned, and Madame Chiang Kai-shek was an alumna! I did not get into Wellesley College. But I knew I wanted to stay close to Nicole and my dad. I wasn't good enough at school to be a doctor or a lawyer, but business was in my blood. I applied to Babson College, which featured a top entrepreneurship undergraduate program—plus, it was close to home.

Even though it was only a twelve-minute drive from our house, my dad said I had to live on campus for the full experience. I really enjoyed the classes; they came naturally to me. A lot of my friends were international students—I think I felt drawn to them from my international travels with my dad growing up. Their backgrounds and cultural differences fascinated me, and their drive to succeed in a foreign country motivated me. At first, we visited the food hall together, but they quickly stopped going; they simply could not stomach the food. I understood why: my stomach hurt every night. Sophomore year, I decided that I wasn't going back to the food hall, and I refused to have my parents pay for it. I asked my aunt for a doctor's note indicating I had strict dietary restrictions, submitted it to the college, and received a check for the year's meal plan. Freedom!

I decided I would cook for myself. I budgeted my food cost per week and started shopping in Wellesley, heading to the local cheese shop, Italian specialty grocer, fish market, and Bread & Circus with my boyfriend. We cooked in the dorm's common area kitchen every night, often setting off the fire alarm. We researched elaborate dishes from fine dining restaurants; I think we were some of the only college kids out there trying to master dishes from The French Laundry cookbook, smashing lobster shells to get the most concentrated lobster bisque.

At least once a week, I'd eat dinner at Sally Ling's in Newton. My dad would ask me to join him for dinner, saying, "Just come by for a quick meal!" I figured it saved me some money and the effort of cooking, and I liked going to see my dad. Those quick dinners almost always turned into late nights, closing down the restaurant as we talked and talked. And every Sunday, without fail, I would head home to do my laundry and eat brunch with dad and Nicole. I loved to have the chance to cook them something new.

Nicole and I still spent our summers with my mom in New Jersey. During the day, I interned, and at night I worked at Sally Ling's, Fort Lee, assisting the general manager. I was adamant that I make my own spending money, as my parents covered the costs for my college tuition. I considered myself very lucky to not have to borrow money for school.

My college life was very full. I made lasting and meaningful friendships while still spending a lot of time with family. My senior year of college, I began to date Kyle again, which made me so happy I felt I was floating. When I graduated, I didn't want to go into finance like everyone else from Babson. My friends were moving to Manhattan to be analysts for fancy banks or working for a family company back in their home countries. I told my dad I thought I should go into the restaurant business, but he suggested it was only because it was in my comfort zone. When I told him I was considering becoming a restaurant consultant, he laughed. "You've never run a restaurant! No one is going to take advice from a twenty-one-year-old." He was right, of course.

I started applying for entry-level jobs. I got unattractive offers for management training programs in Boston and Providence; I wasn't interested. There was a big part of me that still felt like I was a kid: how could I move out on my own? I was always family-oriented, and I had no interest in moving to a new city to live by myself. So, I did the next logical thing: I moved in with my mom in New Jersey. The last time I lived with my mom full-time, I was eleven years old. I wanted to get to know her better and create a closer connection. I packed up my car, drove to New Jersey, and started to look for a job. I knew I could work at Sally Ling's to make money for the time being. Plus, as my dad always said in Chinese: "You must ride a horse to find a horse."

I liked fashion, so I decided to try to find a job in that industry. My first job out of college was for a jewelry designer on Fifth Avenue. We were introduced through a friend of my father's, and it was a complete disaster. She was highly creative, but also very scattered. Her business was a mess, and so was she. I helped her organize her office, paid her long overdue bills, and helped her sell art and jewelry. It was a terrible job, and I only lasted three months. I was back at the beginning of my job search once again. A friend of mine convinced me to apply for a finance job at his company (the exact kind of job I'd avoided). During my interview, I told the managing director that my worst class at Babson was finance. I wasn't going to lie! (Under promise, over deliver.) But he quizzed me and said that I knew more than the average entry-level analyst. I was hired with a nice signing bonus. My dad was so proud, thinking that this job would serve as a great foundation for my career. I wasn't so sure, but the money was good!

During my time at Standard & Poor's Corporate Value Consulting group, I would spend most of my time reading the food section of the New York Times. I researched the best burger, the best donut, and the top restaurants in New York, making a schedule to hit all the top food destinations. I was so incredibly bored that I went into the office of the director of International Expansion and asked for a new opportunity. I told him that I spoke fluent Chinese and suggested that I could help with international projects. This was a great move—he

sent me to Asia to accompany a managing director from the Philadelphia office for two weeks. The best part, of course, was the food. We visited Thailand, Indonesia, Malaysia, and China. I looked for the best of the best in each city we visited and photographed everything I ate. Thank goodness for expense accounts!

Kyle and I were dating long-distance, and so I drove back and forth between New Jersey and Boston often, just as I did during my grade-school years. Even though I wanted to hang out with Kyle every weekend, I split the

weekend between spending time with Kyle and seeing my family. I knew I might be with Kyle for the rest of my life, but I would not have my dad forever. His plan to move back to China after Nicole's graduation made it even more important that I spend as much time with him as possible.

After a year of commuting, I decided it was time to move into the city on my own. At the same time, Kyle also moved to New York for his new real estate job. Knowing that he was just a few blocks away made the move all the better, and we dove right into big city living. I spent every dollar I made on food—hosting dinner parties, dining out, grabbing drinks with friends... I lived like every other analyst in New York, not saving a penny! (I did, in fact, eventually run out of money.)

After five years in finance, I knew that it was not going to be my future. I knew I could no longer deny that I loved food, restaurants, and hospitality. I needed to officially join the industry to learn more. Although I had spent my whole life working in my parents' many restaurants, I'd never managed one. So, I took the leap

and asked my mom if I could learn how to manage Sally Ling's, Fort Lee.

When I called my dad in China to tell him the news, I was surprised to hear he thought it was a good idea. (I think our parents know us better than we think they do.) My mom was happy to have the help and welcomed me with open arms. It felt like I was starting over again, but this time, I had a better understanding of food and what made me happy. Kyle was supportive and wanted me to explore my passion. I was ready to jump in.

During my two years managing Sally Ling's, Fort Lee, I learned a lot about what I liked and didn't like about the restaurant business:

- I didn't like dealing with alcohol, buying it or selling it.

- The linen bills were never accurate.

- Servers were never working happily and were always competitive.

- Finding good people and training them was challenging.

- Relying on an executive chef to make his sauces was suffocating.

- The menu was too expansive, the costs were high, and there was a lot of spoilage.

- I realized the most ordered items were the simpler dishes—but we still bought the lobsters and ducks.

Most of all, I realized I loved working with my mom on catering projects, big and small. I watched her approach to planning events with her clients. She was smart and strategic, while also beautiful and feminine. She was tough as nails, and she made it all look so easy (though I know it was often stressful).

My dad was in China, but we continued to talk often. He enjoyed listening to my observations and what I was learning along the way. He urged me to be thoughtful about the restaurant industry, and to make smart choices if I ever took the plunge. He confirmed my suspicions that fine dining profit margins are low, saying that the fancier the restaurant, the bigger the headache. He explained that he and my mom created Sally Ling's in Boston because they were passionate and saw the opportunity at that time and place. He suggested that the best-case scenario for a restaurant owner is to create a concept that could function without them on a day-to-day basis. I valued his opinion and his expertise immensely and cherished these conversations.

But our conversations were cut short. My life changed forever when my dad died suddenly from a brain aneurysm. I was twenty-seven and Nicole was about to turn nineteen. It feels like yesterday that I received that phone call. My dad had the answers to all my questions, and I wasn't sure how I was going to go on. Thankfully, my mom was there to support me. I always knew my mother was a strong person, but it was never more apparent than the days after my father's death. She told us that we were now exclusively hers, as we no longer had our father to lean on. I could see that she felt an enormous responsibility and my heart broke for her too. We all lost something that day.

I am so thankful for my time with my father. I feel so lucky that I got to know him as a person, and not just as my dad. My biggest sadness is that he was not able to see me get married or to meet his grandchildren, which was his greatest wish. But his lessons ring as loud and true today as they ever have. I still work hard to make him proud. When he left us physically, I made a promise to myself that I would do what he wished for me. I was going to be the self-sufficient and independent woman he always urged me to be. He lives in me and is with me always.

> *My dad had the answers to all my questions, and I wasn't sure how I was going to go on. Thankfully, my mom was there to support me. I always knew my mother was a strong person, but it was never more apparent than the days after my father's death.*

RICE CAKES SHANGHAI STYLE

上海炒年糕 **Serves 4**

When I was in college, I went to Shanghai at least once a year with my father. These trips were an opportunity to hunt for the best foods, whether they were made by street vendors or in the fanciest restaurants. Sautéed rice cakes, a classic Shanghainese dish, always topped the list of foods to try. Prepare them this way and you'll see why.

1 pound fresh rice cakes (usually sold frozen or refrigerated), soaked overnight

4 ounces boneless, skinless chicken breast, shredded into long thin strips

½ teaspoon cornstarch

1½ teaspoon salt, divided

1 tablespoon vegetable oil, plus more for cooking

4 dry shiitake mushrooms, soaked in warm water for 25 minutes

4 leaves Napa cabbage, thinly shredded (approximately 2 cups)

1 small carrot, peeled and julienned

2 tablespoons chicken broth (can substitute with water)

Prep list

SOAK THE RICE CAKES in 4 cups of cold water overnight or for at least 12 hours.

IN A MEDIUM BOWL, combine the chicken, the cornstarch, ½ teaspoon salt, and 1 tablespoon vegetable oil and mix. Chill for at least 30 minutes in the refrigerator.

REMOVE THE MUSHROOMS from the water. Cut off and discard the stems, and shred thinly.

PREPARE AND MEASURE the remaining ingredients.

Cooking

Heat a medium non-stick skillet over medium heat. When the pan is warm, add 1 tablespoon of the oil. When the oil is hot, add the chicken and cook until it just turns white, 1 to 2 minutes. Remove and set aside.

Heat the same pan over medium heat. Add 3 tablespoons of the oil. When the oil is hot, add the vegetables and ½ teaspoon of the salt and cook for about 4 minutes, mixing well. Add the rice cakes, the chicken, the chicken broth, and the remaining ½ teaspoon of salt. Cook until the rice cakes soften, another 4 to 5 minutes, stirring continuously. Remove from heat, season to taste.

ANTS CLIMBING ON A TREE

螞蟻上樹 **Serves 4**

This dish is a favorite from my childhood. I always thought it was such a strange and wonderful name. This is a classic Sichuan dish—it's spicy, delicious, and satisfying. As I get older, I appreciate the simplicity of it. The vermicelli soaks up the delicious sauce and the heat comes from peppercorn and chili sauce.

Sauce

¼ cup chicken broth

2 tablespoons sriracha or another spicy chili sauce

2 tablespoons soy sauce

1 tablespoon sugar

1 teaspoon sesame oil

½ teaspoon Peppercorn Oil, pg. 46

3 tablespoons vegetable oil

6 ounces ground pork

8 ounces dry bean thread vermicelli, soaked in warm water for 30 minutes

2 tablespoons Preserved Mustard Greens

2 scallions, trimmed and chopped

Prep list

MAKE THE SAUCE: In a small bowl, combine the sauce ingredients and mix well.

IN A SMALL BOWL, combine the sesame oil and the Peppercorn Oil.

PREPARE AND MEASURE the remaining ingredients.

Cooking

Heat a medium pan over medium heat. Once the pan is warm, add the vegetable oil. When the oil is hot, add the pork, mixing well to break it up into smaller pieces. Cook until the pork begins to brown, about 2 minutes.

Add the vermicelli, the sauce, and the preserved mustard greens and cook until the sauce is absorbed, about 1 minute. Remove from heat, add the oil mixture, and stir well. Garnish with the chopped scallions.

Serve and enjoy!

BEEF WITH ASPARAGUS

芦笋牛肉 **Serves 4**

Beef with broccoli has long been a go-to American Chinese classic. This dish is similar, but possibly a bit more elegant. At least, that's how I felt when I would cook it in the shared kitchen of my college dorm or in my tiny Manhattan apartment. It's a crowd pleaser for meat lovers, while also sneaking in a bit of nutrition with the crunchy asparagus. Enjoy it over steamed white rice.

1 pound flank steak

Marinade

2 tablespoons oyster sauce

2 tablespoons Shaoxing rice wine

1 teaspoon dark soy sauce

1 teaspoon cornstarch

½ teaspoon sugar

¼ teaspoon ginger powder

3 tablespoons vegetable oil

---

3 tablespoons vegetable oil

1 bunch fresh asparagus (about 1 pound), trimmed and cut on a bias into 2½-inches long pieces

2 to 3 cloves garlic, peeled and thinly sliced

½ teaspoon sea salt

Freshly ground black pepper

Prep list

PLACE THE FLANK STEAK in the freezer for about 45 minutes. When it's icy cold but still bendable, cut across the grain into 3- by 2- by ¼-inch slices.

MAKE THE MARINADE: In a medium bowl, combine the marinade ingredients, add the steak, and mix well. Marinate for at least 30 minutes in the refrigerator.

PREPARE AND MEASURE the remaining ingredients.

Cooking

Heat a large pan over high heat. Once the pan is hot, add 3 tablespoons of the oil. When it shimmers, add the asparagus and the garlic and cook until the asparagus is tender but still crispy, about 2 minutes. Remove from the pan and sprinkle with the salt.

Return the same pan to high heat. Once the pan is hot, add the beef. Cook until the beef just starts turning brown, about 2 minutes. Add back the asparagus and mix well. Add 6 turns of freshly ground black pepper. Cook for about 1 to 2 minutes more, making sure not to overcook the beef.

To trim the stringy, stalky stems off asparagus, hold each end and snap to break. The asparagus will split at a natural point, separating the stem from the tender tip.

CHICKEN WITH MUSHROOMS IN OYSTER SAUCE

磨菇鸡片 **Serves 4**

I'd never had this dish before I worked the front of the house at Sally Ling's, Fort Lee. I marveled at the tenderness of the chicken and how it blended with the earthy flavor of the mushrooms. If you love mushrooms (as I do), you'll love this dish. It pairs wonderfully with a light vegetable side like Baby Bok Choy with Fresh Garlic (pg. 167) or Wok Roasted String Beans with Preserved Mustard Greens (pg. 177).

1 pound boneless, skinless chicken breast sliced into 2- by 1- by ⅛-inch pieces

Marinade

2 tablespoons vegetable oil

1½ teaspoons salt

1½ teaspoons soy sauce

1 teaspoon cornstarch, plus more for slurry

Sauce

½ cup chicken broth

2 tablespoons Shaoxing rice wine

2 tablespoons oyster sauce

2 teaspoons sugar

2 tablespoons vegetable oil

5 fresh garlic cloves, peeled and crushed

8 ounces mushrooms, sliced into ¼-inch thick pieces

Prep list

MAKE THE MARINADE: In a medium bowl, combine the marinade ingredients, add the chicken, and mix well. Marinate for at least 30 minutes in the refrigerator.

MAKE THE SAUCE: In a small bowl, combine the sauce ingredients and mix.

MAKE A CORNSTARCH SLURRY: In a small bowl, combine 1 tablespoon of cornstarch with 3 tablespoons of water, mixing until smooth. If the cornstarch and water separate over time, you may need to mix again before using.

PREPARE AND MEASURE the remaining ingredients.

Cooking

Heat a large pan over high heat. Once the pan is hot, add 2 tablespoons of the oil. When it shimmers, add the garlic and toast until golden, about 30 seconds. Remove and discard the garlic.

Reduce heat to medium, add the marinated chicken, and cook until just turned white, about 2 minutes. Add the mushrooms and cook until tender, about 2 minutes more. Add the sauce and cook for about 30 seconds. Add the cornstarch slurry and cook until the sauce thickens, about 1 minute.

COLD NOODLES WITH SESAME SAUCE

芝麻涼麵 **Serves 4**

Who doesn't love this classic Chinese take-out dish? When I was in college, I'd eat it right out of the box and throw in an extra order for late night. But don't be fooled—this dish isn't just for late night. Cold sesame noodles make a great appetizer at your next dinner party, or a side dish during a summer BBQ. Any noodle will work here (in a pinch, try instant ramen or spaghetti), but my preference is a Chinese White Noodle—wheat based and straight. Put your own spin on it: Add any type of shredded vegetables or protein that you have on hand. The key is to finely shred whatever you're adding to match the size of the noodles. Add snow peas, carrots, celery, farm fresh lettuce, cabbage, chicken, firm tofu, or shredded pork. The list goes on!

8 ounces dry white noodles

1 cup bean sprouts

Sauce

¾ cup Sesame Sauce, pg. 42

2 cloves garlic, peeled
  and minced

1 tablespoon sesame oil

1 tablespoon Dumpling
  Daughter Spicy Sweet Soy
  (optional)

1 tablespoon black vinegar

4-inch piece English cucumber,
  cut into matchsticks

2 scallions, trimmed
  and chopped

Prep list

COOK THE NOODLES according to package instructions and rinse under cold water. Strain the noodles thoroughly, making sure there is not much residual water.

CLEAN UP THE BEAN SPROUTS by removing and discarding any imperfect ends, then blanch the sprouts in boiling water for 1 minute and drain thoroughly.

MAKE THE SAUCE: In a medium bowl, combine the sauce ingredients and whisk until it is a smooth paste.

PREPARE AND MEASURE the remaining ingredients.

Plating

Add the cooked noodles and the sauce to a large serving bowl. Toss until the sauce is evenly distributed throughout the noodles. Place the cucumbers and the bean sprouts on top of the noodles and garnish with the scallions—then dig in.

FIRM TOFU WITH CHINESE CHIVES & VEGETABLES

韭菜豆干 **Serves 2**

Albeit simple, this dish will impress guests and friends. You may have to go to a Chinese market to find five spice tofu and fresh Chinese chives, but the effort is worth it. The resulting dish is beautiful, refined, and delicious—even though it takes just minutes to pull together. This is one of my favorite vegetarian entrées. Make sure to cut the tofu, celery, peppers, and chives so they are all similar in size.

1 package five spice tofu (12 ounces), sliced into 2½-inch matchsticks

3 small stalks celery, julienned into 2½-inch pieces

½ bell pepper, julienned into 2½-inch pieces

1-inch bundle Chinese chives, cut into 2½-inch pieces

2 tablespoons oyster sauce

1 tablespoon soy sauce

2 tablespoons vegetable oil

Prep list

IN A SMALL BOWL, combine the oyster sauce and the soy sauce and mix.

PREPARE AND MEASURE the remaining ingredients.

Cooking

Heat a medium pan over medium heat. Once the pan is hot, add the oil. When it shimmers, add the peppers and the celery and cook until tender, about 2 minutes. Add the chives, the tofu, and the sauce. Cook until all the ingredients are tender and warmed through, about 2 minutes more.

Serve over rice and enjoy!

GRAND MARNIER SHRIMP

果汁大蝦 **Serves 4**

In the old days, a Chinese restaurant would feature the cuisine of the chef's province. My parents made a bold decision to introduce several regional styles when they first opened Sally Ling's, picking the best dishes from the Mandarin, Sichuan, Cantonese, and Taiwanese traditions. Today, this is a common practice, but it was nothing short of a revelation when they started out. I am not sure of the origin of this dish, though it has always been popular at Cantonese restaurants. Typically, it's prepared with candied walnuts, but our version omits them. Using sparkling water in the batter is a great way to get everything extra crispy and light. Once you learn how to fry with tempura batter, you'll want to try it again and again.

1 pound shrimp (16-20 per pound)

Tempura Batter

1 cup all-purpose flour

1 cup sparkling water (or substitute with still water if necessary)

½ cup ice water

1 egg

1 tsp salt

Sauce

¼ cup mayonnaise

¼ cup sweetened condensed milk

1 tablespoon orange marmalade

Zest of 1 orange

Juice of ½ lemon

1 tablespoon Grand Marnier or Cointreau

¼ cup cornstarch

3 cups vegetable oil, for frying

Prep list

PEEL AND DEVEIN THE SHRIMP, then rinse with cold water. Pat the shrimp dry with a paper towel.

MAKE THE TEMPURA BATTER: In a medium bowl, combine the tempura batter ingredients and mix.

MAKE THE SAUCE: In a medium bowl, combine the sauce ingredients and mix.

LINE A BAKING SHEET with paper towels for the crispy shrimp.

Cooking

In a medium bowl, toss the shrimp and the cornstarch, evenly coating the shrimp. Remove from the bowl, shaking off any excess cornstarch. Dredge the shrimp in the tempura batter, making sure to evenly coat all sides.

Over medium heat, bring the oil to 350°F in a medium sauce pot. (A pot about 6 to 8 inches in diameter works best; you will require less oil and limit the mess.)

Gently place the shrimp in the oil, moving them around to prevent them from sticking together. Cook until the batter is slightly crisp and the shrimp are light pink, about 2 minutes. Remove with a slotted spoon and transfer to the prepared baking sheet to remove excess oil. Fry in batches of 4 to 5 shrimp.

Place the shrimp on a platter and pour the sauce over the top.

HOMESTYLE EGGS WITH TOMATOES

蕃茄炒蛋   **Serves 4**

Scrambled eggs? With fresh, ripe tomatoes? Heaven! I learned to love the versatility of this dish in college, cooking in the common kitchen of the dormitory. I had it with my morning congee, my lunch noodles, or as a shared dish during a dinner with friends. No tomatoes? Use scallions. If you have a sweet tooth, try the ketchup, but if you prefer your eggs to be a bit more savory, feel free to omit it. The key is that this dish is easy, satisfying comfort food.

5 large eggs

½ teaspoon salt

4 tablespoons vegetable oil, divided

2 medium tomatoes, roughly chopped into 1-inch pieces

2 tablespoons ketchup (optional)

1 teaspoon sugar

Prep list

IN A MEDIUM BOWL, whisk the eggs together with the salt.

PREPARE AND MEASURE the remaining ingredients.

Cooking

Heat a medium pan over high heat. Add 2 tablespoons of the oil. When it's hot, add the eggs and scramble quickly, stirring constantly, until cooked through, about 45 seconds. Remove the eggs from the pan to a serving plate.

Return the pan to high heat. Add the remaining 2 tablespoons of oil. When it's hot, add the tomatoes, the ketchup (if using), and the sugar. Cook for about 2 minutes, stirring occasionally to prevent sticking, until the tomatoes are tender. Add the scrambled eggs back to the pan and stir to incorporate.

CHINESE CHIVES WITH EGGS

韭菜炒鸡蛋 **Serves 4**

This is an East-meets-West omelet that I often made for friends in college. Chinese chives (occasionally called Garlic Chives) are a unique aromatic herb. They differ from their French cousins in that they are larger and have a stronger flavor. This dish is good enough to eat on its own during a quiet night in, but fancy enough for a dinner party. Left to my own devices, I fold the eggs between two slices of bread, making the best breakfast sandwich ever.

5 large eggs, whisked in a small bowl

½ teaspoon salt

1 cup fresh Chinese chives, chopped into ½-inch batons

2 tablespoons vegetable oil

Prep list

SPRINKLE THE SALT AND THE CHIVES into the eggs and mix until incorporated.

PREPARE AND MEASURE the remaining ingredients.

Cooking

Heat a medium pan over medium heat. Once the pan is hot, add the oil. Check to see if the oil is hot enough by adding a little bit of egg—if it sizzles, it's ready. Then add the remaining egg mixture. The outer edges will cook faster than the middle. As the edges begin to cook, gently push the cooked edges in toward the center, but resist scrambling the eggs. You are looking for evenly cooked, larger pieces. Cook for about 2 minutes, but not much more; aim for tender, not overcooked. Try this as a side dish or a breakfast sandwich!

KUNG PAO CHICKEN

宫保鸡丁   **Serves 4**

I once called a Sichuan restaurant and ordered in Mandarin. When I asked for Kung Pao Chicken, the man on the other end asked, "American or Chinese style?" I appreciated the question—I wanted it Chinese style.

Kung Pao Chicken is a classic Sichuan chicken dish with variations all over the world. The Americanized version has a heavy savory and spicy sauce, but the authentic version is dry and has more heat than the average person can take. This recipe is made in the traditional style—tender chicken thighs cooked with a generous amount of dried chili peppers and peanuts. In my opinion, it's the only way to make the dish. Dial down the heat by using fewer dried chilis, and whatever you do, don't eat them. There's a ton of flavor here—a bowl of white rice is a must!

1 pound boneless skinless
   chicken thighs

Marinade

1 tablespoon soy sauce

2 teaspoons hoisin sauce

½ teaspoon sugar

½ teaspoon salt

1 teaspoon cornstarch

2 tablespoons vegetable oil

1 heaping cup dried Sichuan
   chili peppers, soaked in 1½
   cups water for at least 1 hour

2 tablespoons vegetable
   oil, divided

1 scallion, trimmed
   and chopped

3 cloves garlic, peeled and
   thinly sliced

¼ cup unsalted peanuts

1 tablespoon Shaoxing rice wine

3 dashes white pepper

Prep list

TRIM EXCESS FAT from the chicken and slice into 1-inch cubes.

MAKE THE MARINADE: In a medium bowl, combine the marinade ingredients, add the chicken, and mix well. Marinate for at least 30 minutes in the refrigerator.

STRAIN THE PEPPERS from the water after soaking. (Soaking is what brings out the spice of the peppers.)

PREPARE AND MEASURE the remaining ingredients.

Cooking

Heat a large pan over medium heat. Once the pan is hot, add 1 tablespoon of the oil. When it's hot, add the marinated chicken and cook until just turning color, about 4 to 5 minutes. Remove and set aside on the serving platter.

Heat the same pan over high heat. Add the remaining 1 tablespoon of oil, then add the scallions, the garlic, and the chili peppers and stir-fry, constantly shaking the pan, until the garlic is toasted and the aroma is spicy, about 2 minutes. Add the chicken, the peanuts, and the rice wine. Season with a few dashes of the white pepper. Toss to evenly distribute, cooking everything throughout. Serve with rice.

SHREDDED LAMB WITH SCALLIONS

葱爆羊肉 **Serves 4**

This refined and light approach to lamb was developed at Sally Ling's. In Western cultures, lamb is often a spring meal, but the Chinese believe that it's a perfect dish when you're cold or in need of strength, as it's believed that lamb promotes warmth. I crave this recipe during the fall and winter. I like to complement it with a hearty side dish, like Homestyle Eggs with Tomato (pg. 118) or Mom's Eggplant (pg. 160).

½ pound lamb loin
  or tenderloin

Marinade

1 tablespoon hoisin sauce

1 tablespoon vegetable oil

2 teaspoons oyster sauce

2 teaspoons Shaoxing rice wine

2 teaspoons soy sauce

½ teaspoon sugar

½ teaspoon Worcestershire
  sauce

½ teaspoon cornstarch

2 tablespoons vegetable oil

½-inch piece fresh ginger root,
  peeled and julienned

5 scallions, trimmed, halved
  lengthwise, and cut into
  3-inch pieces

¼ teaspoon black pepper or 6
  turns freshly ground pepper

Prep list

TRIM EXCESS FAT from the lamb. Shred the lamb by slicing across the grain into thin, 2-inch long pieces, about ⅛-inch thick. Stack the pieces, then cut vertically through the stack, against the grain, into thin shreds.

MAKE THE MARINADE: In a medium bowl, combine the marinade ingredients, add the lamb, and mix well. Marinate for at least 30 minutes in the refrigerator.

PREPARE AND MEASURE the remaining ingredients.

Cooking

Heat a large pan over medium heat. Once the pan is hot, add 2 tablespoons of the oil. When it shimmers, add the ginger and cook until golden, about 1 minute.

Add the marinated lamb and cook until just cooked through, about 3 minutes. Add the scallions and the black pepper. Cook until the scallions have wilted, about 2 minutes more.

MA-PO SPICY TOFU

麻婆豆腐 **Serves 4**

My first job out of college was in finance. At lunch, my co-workers and I would often go to a restaurant called the China Chalet, where I'd order this dish. None of my male co-workers could handle the heat—when done right, the spice of Ma-Po should excite and thrill you. I'd go back to the office satisfied, sweaty—and energized. Meanwhile my co-workers had to have another cup of coffee. Ma-Po can be served with rice as a traditional meal or, if you're feeling creative, on top of noodles or salad. Add extra Peppercorn Oil if you like the tingly, mouth-numbing feeling—or if you're just looking for an even bigger endorphin kick!

½ pound ground pork

Marinade

1 teaspoon soy sauce

1 teaspoon cornstarch, plus more for slurry

Sauce

2 tablespoons doubanjiang (Sichuan hot bean sauce)

¾ cup chicken stock or water

1 tablespoon Shaoxing rice wine

1 teaspoon sugar

3 tablespoons vegetable oil

1 large clove garlic, peeled and minced

1 package soft tofu (16 ounces), diced into ¾-inch cubes

1 teaspoon Peppercorn Oil, pg. 46

1 scallion, only the greens, trimmed and chopped

Prep list

MAKE THE MARINADE: In a medium bowl, combine the marinade ingredients with 1 tablespoon water, add the pork, and mix well. Marinate for at least 30 minutes in the refrigerator.

MAKE THE SAUCE: In a small bowl, combine the Ma-Po sauce ingredients and mix.

MAKE A CORNSTARCH SLURRY: In a small bowl, combine 1 teaspoon of cornstarch with 2 tablespoons of water, mixing until smooth. If the cornstarch and water separate over time, you may need to mix again before using.

PREPARE AND MEASURE the remaining ingredients.

Cooking

Heat a large pan over medium heat. Once the pan is hot, add the vegetable oil. When it shimmers, add the garlic and toast until golden, about 30 seconds. Add the pork, breaking it apart into small pieces. Cook until the pork begins to brown, about 1 to 2 minutes.

Add the Ma-Po sauce and the tofu. Gently stir to incorporate all the ingredients by pushing away from you so that you don't break apart the tofu. Reduce the heat to medium-low, cover, and simmer for 6 to 8 minutes.

Slowly add the cornstarch slurry and cook until the sauce thickens, about 1 minute.

Add the Peppercorn Oil and gently fold in to mix well. Plate and garnish with the chopped scallions.

SACHA BEEF WITH TOMATOES

沙茶蕃茄牛 **Serves 4**

Mark my words: sacha will be the next big thing in the sauce world—it's only a matter of time until it becomes a household name. This sauce is a secret weapon for big flavor, and it lasts for months in the fridge. Made of oil, garlic, shallots, dried shrimp, chili, and other savory ingredients, it's spicy and deliciously savory. Though it's often described as Chinese BBQ sauce, I don't think that does the taste justice. This dish is just one example of how to showcase sacha. I would pair this with fried rice or light vegetables to balance the richness.

1 pound flank steak

Marinade

4 tablespoons sacha sauce

2 tablespoons Shaoxing
   rice wine

2 teaspoons oyster sauce

2 teaspoons dark soy sauce

1 teaspoon cornstarch

1 tablespoon vegetable oil

2 tablespoons vegetable oil

6 cloves garlic, peeled and
   thinly sliced

1 medium onion, chopped into
   1-inch wedges lengthwise,
   then cut in half (about 1 cup)

2 medium tomatoes, roughly
   chopped into 1-inch wedges
   (about 2 cups)

1 tablespoon sugar

Prep list

PLACE THE FLANK STEAK in the freezer for about 45 minutes. When it's icy cold but still bendable, slice across the grain into 3- by 2- by ¼-inch thick pieces.

MAKE THE MARINADE: In a medium bowl, combine the marinade ingredients, add the flank steak, and mix well. Marinate for at least 1 hour in the refrigerator.

PREPARE AND MEASURE the remaining ingredients.

Cooking

Heat a large pan over high heat. Once the pan is hot, add 2 tablespoons of the oil. When it shimmers, add the garlic and toast until golden, about 30 seconds. Reduce the heat to medium and add the onions and the tomatoes. Cook until the onions are slightly tender, about 2 to 3 minutes. Add the sugar, toss, and transfer to a serving plate.

Heat the same pan over high heat. When the pan is hot, add the marinated flank steak. Cook until the beef begins to brown, about 2 minutes. Return the tomatoes and the onions to the pan and cook about 2 minutes more. Remove the beef and the vegetables with a slotted spoon (if there is residual oil, you can leave that in the pan).

SALLY LING'S FRIED RICE

本楼炒飯 **Serves 4 to 6**

Thirty years ago, and even up until today, most of the fried rice dishes made in Chinese American restaurants were very dark in color, the result of lots of soy sauce. Not at Sally Ling's. My parents' restaurant was known for a fried rice that was very light in color, and we continue making it this way at Dumpling Daughter today. At first glance, people might think that the dish will be bland since they're used to the kind laden with soy sauce. I too never understood why this recipe was so good until I learned to make it myself.

Every ingredient is delicately cooked to perfection, seasoned along the way, and tied together at the end for the full effect. It may take time to prepare, but this dish is so good it can stand alone. It's definitely worth the effort!

Please note: this makes a large amount of fried rice. You may have leftovers. You will be happy about this!

12 shrimp (21-25 per pound)

2 medium eggs, whisked in a small bowl

6 tablespoons vegetable oil, divided

1½ teaspoons salt, divided

4 ounces boneless, skinless chicken breast, shredded into thin strips

½ onion, peeled and diced (about ½ cup)

1 cup frozen peas and carrots

2 ounces ham steak, cut into small cubes

4 cups white rice, cooked

2 scallions, only the greens, trimmed and chopped

Prep list

PEEL AND DEVEIN THE SHRIMP, then rinse with cold water. Pat the shrimp dry with a paper towel.

PREPARE AND MEASURE the remaining ingredients.

Cooking

Heat a large pan over high heat. Once the pan is hot, add 2 tablespoons of the oil. When it shimmers, add the eggs and scramble until just cooked, about 1 minute. Sprinkle with a third of the salt and transfer to the serving platter you plan to use.

Heat the same pan over medium heat. When the pan is hot, add 2 tablespoons of the oil. Add the shrimp and the chicken and cook until both are cooked through, about 2 minutes. Transfer to the serving platter with the eggs and sprinkle with a third of the salt.

Heat the same pan over medium heat. When the pan is hot, add the remaining 2 tablespoons of oil. Add the onions and the peas and carrots and cook until they are soft, about 1 to 2 minutes. Add the ham and the rice. Return the chicken, the shrimp, and the eggs to the pan.

Mix to break up the rice and evenly incorporate all the ingredients. Sprinkle the remaining salt over the dish and cook until all the ingredients are warmed up. Remove from heat, add the scallions, and mix well. Serve on a large platter or bowl.

SHRIMP SHANGHAINESE STYLE

干烧虾 **Serves 4**

This is another legendary dish from Sally Ling's, Fort Lee. It requires only a few ingredients, but it's a crowd pleaser. The shrimp are tender, yet crisp, bathed in a sweet and sour sauce with spicy ginger. You won't believe how easy it is to make and how quickly it disappears once it hits the table.

1 pound shrimp (under 12
    per pound)

Sauce

1-inch piece fresh ginger root,
    peeled and minced

¼ cup ketchup

3 tablespoons sugar

1 tablespoon Shaoxing rice wine

2 teaspoons white vinegar

½ lemon, juiced

¼ teaspoon salt

1 teaspoon cornstarch

3 tablespoons vegetable oil

1 medium onion, peeled and
    diced into ½-inch pieces

1 scallion, only the greens,
    trimmed and chopped

Prep list

PEEL AND DEVEIN THE SHRIMP, then rinse with cold water. Pat the shrimp dry with a paper towel.

MAKE THE SAUCE: In a medium bowl, combine the sauce ingredients and mix.

MAKE A CORNSTARCH SLURRY: In a small bowl, combine 1 teaspoon of cornstarch with 2 tablespoons of water, mixing until smooth. If the cornstarch and water separate over time, you may need to mix again before using.

PREPARE AND MEASURE the remaining ingredients.

Cooking

Heat a large pan over medium-high heat. Once the pan is hot, add the oil. When it shimmers, add the onions and cook until translucent, about 3 minutes. Add the shrimp and cook until pink, about a minute, flipping halfway through, being careful not to brown the onions.

Add the sauce, reduce heat to medium and cook for about 30 seconds. Add the cornstarch slurry and cook until the sauce thickens, about 45 seconds.

Plate and garnish with the chopped scallion greens.

JUMBO SHRIMP WITH BLACK BEAN SAUCE

豆豉大蝦 **Serves 4**

My mom insisted I put this recipe in the book because Americans love black bean sauce. She knows what she's talking about—the restaurant used to sell black bean sauce "on the side" by the pint. The chef made it fresh just for that purpose. The only trick here is to make sure you get the right fermented black beans—dòuchǐ—not the dried black beans you may already have on hand. Use our pantry section as a guide (pg. 18) when you go to your local Chinese market.

1 pound jumbo shrimp (under 12 per pound)

1 red bell pepper, sliced into 1-inch wide strips and then cut into diamonds about 1½ inches in size

1 small yellow onion, cut lengthwise into 1-inch wide wedges and then in half

1 scallion, trimmed and chopped

2 tablespoons Shaoxing rice wine

1 tablespoon soy sauce

1 teaspoon sugar

4 tablespoons vegetable oil, divided

2 tablespoons dòuchǐ (fermented black beans), soaked overnight, rinsed, and roughly chopped

3 cloves garlic, peeled and minced

½-inch piece fresh ginger root, peeled and minced

Prep list

PEEL AND DEVEIN THE SHRIMP, then rinse with cold water. Pat the shrimp dry with a paper towel.

IN A MEDIUM BOWL, combine the bell pepper, the onions, the scallions, the wine, the soy sauce, and the sugar. Mix well.

PREPARE AND MEASURE the remaining ingredients.

Cooking

Heat a large pan over high heat. Once the pan is hot, add 2 tablespoons of the oil. When it shimmers, add the black beans, the garlic, and the ginger. Cook until the garlic and the ginger are lightly browned and aromatic, about 45 seconds. Add the shrimp and cook until pink, about 1 to 2 minutes. Remove the shrimp and set aside.

Heat the same pan over medium heat. Once the pan is hot, add the remaining 2 tablespoons of oil. When it shimmers, add the remaining ingredients and cook for about 3 minutes. When the vegetables have softened but still retain some crunch, return the shrimp to the pan, toss to coat evenly, and serve.

HOME FRIED CHICKEN

炸鸡球 **Serves 4**

When I was working in Manhattan, fried chicken was becoming "a thing." More specifically, Korean fried chicken was gaining in popularity. After work, I would meet my friends in K-town and enjoy BBQ with soju. After a big dinner, we would go to a nightclub where we drank more and ate Korean rice cake—*tteokbokki*—and fried chicken—*chikin*. No matter how much you ate at dinner you always had room for fried chicken. This is my mother's recipe—she made it one day, and when I ate it, I was instantly transported back to those carefree (and drunken) nights in K-town.

1 pound boneless, skinless
  chicken thighs

Marinade

1-inch piece fresh ginger root,
  peeled and chopped

1 clove garlic, peeled and
  chopped

2 tablespoons fish sauce

2 tablespoons sake

2 teaspoons five spice powder

1 cup potato or tapioca starch

3 cups vegetable oil, for frying

Lemon wedges, for serving

Prep list

TRIM EXCESS FAT from the chicken and cut each thigh into quarters.

MAKE THE MARINADE: In a medium bowl, combine the marinade ingredients, add the chicken, and mix well. Marinate for at least 2 hours in the refrigerator.

IN A MEDIUM BOWL, combine the five spice powder and the potato or tapioca starch and mix.

LINE A BAKING SHEET with paper towels for the finished chicken.

PREPARE AND MEASURE the remaining ingredients.

Cooking

Over medium heat, bring the oil to 375°F in a medium sauce pot. (A pot about 6 to 8 inches in diameter works best; you will require less oil and limit the mess.)

Dip each piece of the marinated chicken into the starch mixture. Press and toss, making sure all sides and surfaces are evenly coated. Shake off any excess starch.

Gently place the chicken in the oil and fry until brown and crispy, about 6 to 7 minutes. Work in smaller batches to avoid crowding the pot. Remove the chicken with a slotted spoon and place on the baking sheet to absorb excess oil.

Serve with the lemon wedges, a stack of napkins, and an ice-cold beer.

HOT POT

THERE'S NOTHING LIKE HOT POT ON A COOL NIGHT—but come to think about it, there's nothing like hot pot on a summer day either! All you have to do is balance the heat of the meal with a cold beer. Hot pot isn't only about the food, but the feeling you get when you're eating it, sitting around a steaming pot of simmering soup with your favorite people and a table of proteins, veggies, noodles, and homemade sauce. The windows fog up from steam and you know you've signed up for an eating marathon. I literally get an adrenaline rush.

Hot pot (火锅, Huǒguō) is a staple in Chinese homes and the Far East dining scene. No matter where you are in Asia, you can find a hot pot restaurant. In the Sichuan province, it's a pot of spicy pepper broth; in Taiwan, it's a light chicken broth and the food is prepared and cut in a refined style. If you're unfamiliar with this cooking method, hot pot is a simmering pot of broth in the center of the dining table (similar to Swiss fondue). Dishes of raw ingredients cover the rest of the table. It's an interactive experience that brings everyone at the table together as they cook their own favorites in the delicious broth.

Hot pot is always a fun and delicious meal and remains one of my favorites. Whenever my mom says, "Hot pot?" we all say, "Oh yeah!!!" After a big night of hot pot, I look forward to the next day when I can have the leftovers. I love drinking the soup the day after, as it has so much rich flavor. If there's raw items leftover, you might see me hunched over a simmering pot, indulging on my own.

Everyone can make their own version of hot pot, whether it's a meal for one over the stove or a feast for the whole family around the dining table. For me, the best part is the sauce, and in my opinion, my mom makes the best. I'm honored to share my mom's version of hot pot sauce here, followed by lots of ideas for what to add to your hot pot experience. Have fun!

HOT POT SAUCE

火锅酱   **Yields 1½ cups**

3 tablespoons sugar

½ cup sacha sauce

2 tablespoons sesame oil

¼ cup black vinegar

½ cup soy sauce

¼ cup sesame paste

In a medium bowl, combine the ingredients and whisk until smooth, or use an immersion blender for a faster process.

Ideas for serving:

MEATS & PROTEINS

Thinly sliced beef, lamb, chicken, or pork

Sliced salmon or any white fish that isn't too delicate

Seafood such as prawns, scallops, clams, mussels, crab, lobster, squid (calamari)

Beef tripe

Fish balls

Fish cake

Sausage

Tofu

Chicken feet

Egg

CARBS/STARCHES

Glass noodles (mung bean or rice based)

Dry bean thread vermicelli

Udon noodles

Rice cake (nian gao)

Wontons

VEGETABLES

Baby bok choy

Napa cabbage

Spinach

Mushrooms (shiitake, oyster, king, enoki)

Watercress

Tomato wedges to flavor the soup

CONDIMENTS/SAUCES

Soy sauce

Black vinegar

Cilantro, chopped with stems

Minced garlic

Chopped scallion

Sacha sauce

Chili oil

Minced ginger

THE TRUTH ABOUT MSG

As an owner of a Chinese restaurant, I'm asked about MSG all the time. Customers, the press—it's a topic that has been exhausted over the years, but I've lived with that question since I was a little girl. In middle school, I remember a kid asking me, "Do you use MSG at your restaurants?" (In retrospect, what sixth grader knows about MSG? And then asks a Chinese kid about it?) So I went home and did what I always did: asked my dad. He explained that MSG (monosodium glutamate) is a man-made sodium invented by the Japanese to emulate the flavor of seaweed (which is naturally savory and rich in salt flavor). It's a flavor enhancer and it even occurs naturally in certain foods. He also told me that when Chinese immigrants opened restaurants in the United States, they made food to please the American palates. Believing that Americans loved heavy flavors and food high in sodium, sugar, and oil, they often cooked with MSG, an ingredient that makes everything taste better.

In the late 1960s, following reports that people had bad reactions to food in Chinese restaurants, MSG was suggested to be the culprit. Immediately, MSG became a vilified ingredient in America, creating a cultural fear and backlash against American Chinese food. It even became known as "Chinese restaurant syndrome," a misleading and offensive term. Many restaurants resorted to putting up signs in their windows stating "No MSG" to calm the fears of their customers. But here's the thing: scientists have never been able to find a connection between adverse reactions and the consumption of MSG.

Today, chefs from all around the world use MSG to elevate the flavor of their food. I am willing to bet there is MSG in several packaged foods in your kitchen right now. The stigma remains, but even the FDA says that the ingredient is safe. So, I say, why not try it at home sometime? My mom always says that if you can get your hands on high-quality Japanese MSG, sprinkle just a little at the end of making a seafood dish. The combination of Chinese wine and MSG elevates the dish in a big way. And that's the truth about MSG.

BUILDING A RESTAURANT

Inspired Recipes from the Dumpling Daughter Kitchen

Dumpling Daughter House Fried Rice

Homestyle Moo Shu with Pancakes

**Filet Mignon with Onions, Mushrooms
& Black Pepper Sauce**

Grandma's Beijing Meat Sauce

Scallion Lo Mein

Shrimp with Lobster Sauce (Boston Style)

Coco's Roll-Ups

Eggplant Two Ways:

Mom's Eggplant

Dumpling Daughter Eggplant

Scallion Pancakes

Baby Bok Choy with Fresh Garlic

Crab Rangoons

Dan Dan Mien

Sesame Wontons

**Wok Roasted String Beans with
Preserved Mustard Greens**

**Shredded Pork with
Pickled Mustard Noodle Soup**

Egg Flower Tomato Soup

Beef Beijing Noodle Soup

**Rice Bowls: Choose Your Own
Dumpling Daughter Adventure**

FOR ME, IT HAS ALWAYS BEEN ABOUT THE DUMPLINGS. Dumplings are a through-line in my life—they're always the first thing I'd order in a restaurant or what I'd request at home. Dumplings are labor intensive, so we'd always make huge batches to have ready to go in the freezer. I remember a conversation with my dad, during my college years. We sat together, enjoying a meal of dumplings, of course, and I mused, "If only non-Chinese people would eat dumplings as a meal like we do..." My dad said Americans only saw dumplings as an appetizer and would never be satisfied with only dumplings for a meal. I understood what he meant, but I felt that things could change. Looking back now, I can see that this is where the idea for Dumpling Daughter truly began.

Fast forward to early 2011, during a normal weekend at my mom's house in New Jersey. I was starving and jumped at her offer of dumplings. I could tell that these were not homemade, but they were delicious. I was shocked—and impressed. Where did she get these? She responded that she picked them up in the freezer section at a Chinese supermarket. I could not believe that a machine could make dumplings that were so legit. If it was that easy, then anyone could make dumplings at home.

The next day, I went to the same Hong Kong supermarket in Flushing. I scanned the freezer section and returned home with a dozen different bags of dumplings, including the brand she'd fed me the day before. I cooked them all. It was a real range of results: some didn't look good enough to eat, some had poor instructions, and most were only okay. None were as good as my mom's homemade version—except the brand she'd prepared the day before. They were head and shoulders above the rest. The maker was in Clifton, New Jersey—only twenty minutes away.

I told my mom about the conversation I had with my dad years earlier about dumplings. What did she think? She thought Americans were ready. It could become a "thing." This confirmed my feelings—I was on to something. Then I asked: "What if I distributed them?" And without hesitation, my mom told me that she always dreamed of a food factory business.

The very next day, we followed our Garmin to what looked like a dodgy strip mall, the address leading us to a nameless door with foggy glass. I rang the doorbell. A uniformed older woman came to the door. I explained that I found the dumplings at Hong Kong supermarket and loved them so much that I wanted to sell them. She looked left, right, and back at me, then linked arms with me and pulled me in. On our walk to the office, I saw machines spitting out dumplings and buns. It felt like we were starring in a spy movie. My heart was beating so fast!

The factory's owner had a great product but no marketing skills. I knew this presented a great opportunity and I wanted to be the one to successfully distribute these frozen dumplings to the western market. My parents created something that was so unique and memorable in Boston with Sally Ling's. I wanted to use their legacy to establish a new brand and have their names live on. We eventually bought the factory and asked my older sister, Christina, to take charge of the day-to-day management of our wholesale products.

A few months later, I found myself at a friend's charity event, where I was fortuitously introduced to Stacy Madison of Stacy's Pita Chips. I told her my plan to sell frozen dumplings to western supermarkets and she gave it to me straight: "I get it, your parents started Sally Ling's—but who are you?" Stacy explained I needed a following and a brand before supermarkets would talk to me. Then, the big, scary piece of advice. She told me I should start a restaurant to introduce the product, and to make people want it even more. Well shit, this is exactly what my parents told me never to do! I was to avoid opening my own restaurant at all costs.

I mulled it over. At the time, I lived in Boston with Kyle, now my husband. I had no real job, and I was restless. I needed a project. My dad had left me some money, and I knew I had to use it to create something that would make me self-sufficient, as he always wanted. I decided I was going to open a restaurant. I was doing this.

At the beginning, I believed getting a location would be easy because of my family's legacy. I wrote a business plan and looked for areas in Boston where I thought dumplings and buns would sell. I sat in Harvard Square cafés, counting how many people they served at peak lunch hour. I asked a friend from my finance past to help me with projections from the data I collected. My dream was to open in Harvard Square. Through networking with brokers and meeting well-known landlords, I found a great spot for my unnamed concept. I started emailing with the landlord's representatives—they wanted the business plan, the rendering for the space, and proof of funds. I hired a designer to do renderings, but still needed a name for my concept, and to find more money somewhere. This was a crash course in real estate: I had to learn quickly what it would entail to even be considered in the red hot real estate market in Boston. Ultimately, the landlord decided to gut the entire building and not go ahead with a food concept. This was heartbreaking, but I had learned so much from the process. Now I knew what I needed to make my ideas a reality.

First up: a name. I wanted something that would represent my relation to Sally Ling, and one late night over drinks, my friend suggested "Dumpling Daughter." It's funny to think about now, but I didn't love it initially. Still, it was better than anything I could think of at the time, so I used it as a placeholder in my business plan. I connected with a designer to create a logo. I told the designer what I was envisioning, and twenty-two versions later, we had the Dumpling Daughter mascot. Next, I showed the draft menu to my mom. I wanted to serve all my childhood favorites, as well as dishes I'd tasted while traveling through China with my dad. The business plan now had a name, logo, and menu. We started turning brokers' and landlords' heads, and I began to feel more confident that this was actually going to happen. I talked about my dream of Dumpling Daughter constantly, living and breathing this unborn concept, feeling surges of adrenaline whenever people asked me about it.

But it took SUCH a long time. Pressure mounted as the weeks and months ticked by with no location. Over the course of three years, I had spent so much money on renderings for specific locations, engineering designs, lawyer fees to negotiate leases, and still did not have a lease in place. The doubt and stress started to creep in, and I began to lose hope. My father-in-law warned me that restaurants had a 75% failure rate and urged me to focus on having kids instead. I questioned the plan as well—was this really the best way to get our frozen dumplings into supermarkets? I thought about quitting every day. But I knew that if I didn't follow my passion, I'd regret it. I decided to fight even harder. A restaurant may not have been what my father dreamed for me, but he always advised me to follow my passion.

My parents created something that was so unique and memorable in Boston with Sally Ling's. I wanted to use their legacy to establish a new brand and have their names live on.

In May of 2014, Kyle called me: "My mom was in Weston Center and said that she thinks that the old pizza restaurant space is available. Would you be interested in looking at it?" I said yes without thinking, surprising him with my excitement. My father always dreamed of a fast-casual Chinese restaurant in Weston Center. Dad told me that he approached a landlord back in the 1980s with the concept and the landlord told him no, saying, "People in Weston don't really eat Chinese food." The landlord was probably right: Weston wasn't ready at the time. But things had changed enough to be different this time. I had zero hesitations, and I wanted it without any consideration of the lunch crowds. Weston Center is small and unique; there was no way I could forecast the business from a financial perspective. I asked my mom what she thought about Dumpling Daughter in Weston and she too replied, without hesitation, "I love it." Wow, something my parents actually agreed on. Onward!

With Kyle's help and a very friendly landlord, we had a lease signed in a month. My mom taught me that the most important decision is the location and the landlord, because the landlord is essentially your business partner. When times are tough, the landlord can help or hurt, so it is imperative to have someone you can trust. The lease process was so smooth and so much easier than anything I had dealt with in the last three years that it felt like it was meant to be.

Weston is a quaint and quiet town, its businesses serving the families who live there. I expected locals to trickle in like they would to a gift shop, and that it was going to be fun and relaxing. In the two weeks leading up to my opening, I found paper products and takeout boxes at Restaurant Depot, my mom placed the order with the meat vendor, and the dumplings were shipped and stored in the walk-in freezer. We unwrapped the melamine plates and bowls, organized everything, and worked long days to be ready.

My parents' general manager from Sally Ling's (circa 1988), Johnny Tong, agreed to help me open and manage the restaurant. My parents' waiter from twenty years earlier, Ming, agreed to cook and manage the kitchen. My parents' pastry chef, Sao Shan, now in her 70s, came to help as much as we needed. My mom said it felt like a special reunion—she'd never worked side

by side with them before, only as their boss. The sense of support was immense. I've always been a sentimental person, but this particular moment made my heart full.

We launched Dumpling Daughter on Thursday evening, November 6, 2014. My mom predicted we would sell ten orders of buns and maybe forty orders of dumplings per day, if we were lucky. On opening night, we unlocked the doors. It was freezing outside, and a lady came in to get an order of chicken dumplings and some soup. I wrapped it like it was a gift. I'd packed takeout my whole life, but this order was different because it had my name on it.

We weren't ready for what the second day would bring. We were heavily understaffed and ill-prepared. My mom was wrong. We sold about two hundred orders of dumplings that day. Tickets printed incorrectly; the equipment wasn't working right. It was nothing short of a disaster. Customers were angry and I was stressed. My mother-in-law ran to Bed Bath & Beyond to pick up items that we were clearly missing. I called Kyle for help, and he left his office to work as the cashier and take orders. I'll never forget seeing him walk through the door, wearing his starched collared shirt, wading through the crowd of people waiting to order.

I went home every day and cried...For a guy who never cooked, he was suddenly there, searing pork belly with a blow torch—because it needed to be done.

In Chinese culture, it's good luck to have a grand opening event. We had a big party on Saturday, and I was so happy to see all the friends who had been listening to this idea for years. But I was mostly happy because we didn't open for service that day—Friday had been a nightmare. Later that night, after a few drinks at a French bistro in Boston surrounded by my friends, I began to cry. (The martini likely helped.) I didn't want to go to work the next day. Everything was a mess, and we weren't ready for the crowds. I'd wanted this for years, and now that it was here, I couldn't believe how bad I was at the restaurant business! I'd opened my doors completely unprepared—the pressure was nearly unbearable, and it was my name on the door.

I went home every day and cried. Kyle tried to console me, but also reminded me that I had signed a lease and that I'd worked toward this for years. He told me how proud my dad would be and that my mom was there to support me every step of the way. (But what did he know? He wasn't in deep every day with me in there!) I called him every time I needed him to help. For a guy who never cooked, he was suddenly there, searing pork belly with a blow torch—because it needed to be done. My mother-in-law, a saint, packed takeout for us when she didn't even know what a bun was—because it needed to be done.

The first few weeks could only be described as a shit show—worse because I read the bad reviews on Yelp. One reviewer wrote that we served her a Moo Shu Wrap with Beef, even though she was vegan, and predicted we'd be out of business by spring. We ran out of food every day. I didn't know what a par was. I didn't know that restaurants had inventory standards, so I went every morning to Restaurant Depot to buy ingredients that we ran out of the day before. The dinging sound of new orders coming into the kitchen rang in my ear and gave me anxiety every time. (To this day, when I hear those dings, my heart races.)

I didn't even have a chance to sit and think about a smarter way to do things. It was not supposed to be like this! I thought it was going to be fun, but the reality was far from glamorous. Within the first two weeks, Boston Magazine asked to come in and photograph the dumplings. I was excited but horrified at the same time. This was the plan, right? To market myself as Sally Ling's daughter, reminding people of that legacy so that they'd come and eat our dumplings. But I was overwhelmed and scared.

I closed the restaurant on any day I could to get a day off. I closed on Thanksgiving, Christmas, and New Year's Day, all the days where Chinese restaurants famously do their best business. My mother thought I was crazy. But when I was there, I was filled with dread. I treated everyday like it was a skating competition, as if I was onstage and performing. I lost fifteen pounds and my clothes were falling off me. I cared so deeply about every single customer. When friends of my in-laws came in to congratulate me, I literally looked right through them to see if all the other customers were enjoying their meals. I couldn't focus or relax for a second. I was at a real low point, crying to my mom, when she finally yelled at me: "You asked for this. Now stop crying and get to work!" Then she reminded me that being busy was a good problem to have. "At least you don't have giraffe neck," she said. I thought, "What the heck is giraffe neck?" She explained that giraffe neck is when you sit in your dead restaurant, look at the door, and wait for the next customer to come in. You stare so long, your neck gets long. "Giraffe neck."

These experiences made me realize—yet again—just how strong my mom was. In her own restaurants, my mom never worked in the kitchen. And here she was at my restaurant, doing prep and working as a line cook. She was supposed to be retired, but instead she was with me, experiencing the extreme stress of my new restaurant. During the week of Christmas, we were slammed: the college kids were back in town, and everyone wanted to try Dumpling Daughter. There was a line out the door every day. I remember taking breaks in the walk-in freezer to hide and take some deep

During our busiest moments, I'd catch a glimpse of my mom in the kitchen, working so hard and supporting me in such an incredible way. I knew I had to be the toughest version of myself for her. So, I smiled at everyone and cried in private.

breaths. Once my brain felt frozen over, I'd exit and head right back into the chaos. During our busiest moments, I'd catch a glimpse of my mom in the kitchen, working so hard and supporting me in such an incredible way. I knew I had to be the toughest version of myself for her. So, I smiled at everyone and cried in private.

The new year came, and so did the press—and more customers. On January 14th, *The Boston Globe* published a glowing review written by Sheryl Julian, the most respected food writer in Boston. In the days before it ran, she warned me to prepare extra food, because the crowds would come. We listened to her—but it wasn't enough. We ran out of chicken soup first, then the dumplings. We ultimately sold out of half the menu. I begged Kyle to meet my sister in Connecticut, the halfway point between Weston and the dumpling factory in New Jersey, to bring back a car full of dumplings. As he was driving across state lines, we had to hang a sign on the door stating that we were closed to restock. It was one of the coldest days of winter, and still there were people peering into the windows and knocking on the door. There was a line around the building, and they wanted to be let into the warm restaurant. I felt so uncomfortable, I let them all in—the restaurant filled with people, but I had no food to feed them. It felt like a cafeteria; people wanted to buy any food that was ready, just so they could try Dumpling Daughter.

Those crazy early days never felt rewarding because things never went smoothly. My mom encouraged me, telling me that the crowds were great, but I was still so nervous. Slowly, I began to see that it was working, and that with the right team of people, we were starting to find our stride. My father-in-law, who was always skeptical of my plan, started to show up every day to see the packed restaurant. I knew this signified his approval, something I had always hoped to receive. My mother-in-law was there for me in every way; her willingness to help was limitless. I thought about how my dad would likely critique every decision, but I also knew he would have been so proud. And my mom—wow. We became closer in those days and weeks than ever before. She was my biggest supporter; we spent every day working together from morning to close for months. And Kyle, of course, was there for whatever I needed, talking through my fears and stresses each night. All these people helped define and build Dumpling Daughter.

The road to building Dumpling Daughter was humbling and raw, but eventually, things started to click into place. The return customers gave me confidence. I was now selling Chinese food in the predominantly white town where I grew up; I had built the first ethnic restaurant there to bridge the gap between east and west. I was sharing the food of my childhood, and people loved it.

To this day, one of the most satisfying things about running Dumpling Daughter is watching the kids of my hometown devour dumplings and buns. To see these kids gobbling up my childhood favorites—the very food that used to get me dirty looks at the lunch table—makes me incredibly happy. Today, if a kid brings in Dumpling Daughter leftovers for lunch, the other kids are jealous. I am so proud of the way things have changed. And that boy who made fun of my eyes all those years ago? He's one of the biggest and best supporters of Dumpling Daughter around. (You know who you are!)

DUMPLING DAUGHTER HOUSE FRIED RICE

本楼炒飯   **Serves 4**

The Sally Ling's House Fried Rice was always sautéed, white and light. We simplified the concept at Dumpling Daughter, while making sure to keep the dish refined. Sally Ling's Fried Rice uses shrimp, ham, and mixed vegetables; the Dumpling Daughter version uses Chinese sausage, golden raisins, scallions, and eggs. Chinese sausage is an underutilized ingredient. It is crisp and sweet, with a consistency like chorizo. This recipe is easily doubled to serve more.

4 tablespoons vegetable oil, divided

1 large egg, whisked in a small bowl

1 link Chinese sausage, sliced into ¼-inch thick pieces

2 cups white rice, cooked

½ cup golden raisins

¼ teaspoon salt, plus more to taste

1 scallion, trimmed and chopped

Cooking

Heat a large pan over high heat. Once the pan is hot, add 2 tablespoons of the oil. When it shimmers, add the egg and scramble quickly, stirring constantly, until cooked through. Remove the egg from the pan to a serving platter.

Return the pan to high heat. Add the remaining 2 tablespoons of oil. When it's hot, add the sausage and cook for about 1 minute. Add the rice and mix to break up any clumps. Cook until the rice is warmed through, about 1 minute.

Add the raisins and the salt and cook for about 30 seconds. Add the scallions and the egg and cook for another 30 seconds.

HOMESTYLE MOO SHU WITH PANCAKES

家常菜薄饼 **Serves 4**

My mom is the only person I know who makes Moo Shu pancakes from scratch. She makes the dough fresh and rolls each pancake out, one by one. Then she cooks them on a dry pan, yet again, one by one… The finished product is so thin you can see your hand through it. If you don't have the time to make your own, look for Golden Bowl brand pancakes. As for the filling, American-style Moo Shu typically uses shredded cabbage, which is both inexpensive and widely available. This recipe calls for bean sprouts, which is more authentic and features a great crunch. Traditionally, we enjoy this dish as the main event at dinner, allowing us to fully appreciate all that delicious effort.

12 ounces bean sprouts

4 eggs, whisked in a small bowl

Sauce

3 tablespoons oyster sauce

1 tablespoon Shaoxing rice wine

1 teaspoon sesame oil

―――――

3 tablespoons vegetable oil

3 ounces dry bean thread vermicelli, soaked for 30 minutes in room temperature water

6 ounces five spice tofu (or substitute with extra firm tofu), sliced into matchsticks

10 Chinese chives, trimmed and cut into 2-inch pieces

2 scallions, trimmed, halved lengthwise, and cut into 2-inch pieces

2 teaspoons sugar

1 teaspoon salt

Hoisin sauce

Savory pancakes, store-bought

Prep list

CLEAN UP THE BEAN SPROUTS by removing and discarding any imperfect ends, then soak the sprouts in water to wash and drain.

MAKE THE SAUCE: In a small bowl, combine the sauce ingredients and mix well.

PREPARE AND MEASURE the remaining ingredients.

Cooking

Steam the pancakes according to package instructions. You want them to be hot when you're ready!

Heat a large pan over high heat. Once the pan is hot, add the vegetable oil. When it shimmers, add the eggs and scramble quickly, stirring constantly, until cooked through.

Add the vermicelli, the bean sprouts, the tofu, the chives, and the scallions, then cook until the vegetables have softened, about 2 minutes. Add the sugar and the salt and cook for about 1 minute. Finally, add the sauce and cook until the vegetables are tender, about 1 to 2 minutes more.

To serve, spoon hoisin sauce down the center of a steamed pancake, then place a long mound of the filling on the hoisin sauce. Carefully fold the left edge of the pancake over the vertical mound of stuffing, use your right hand to fold the bottom of the pancake perpendicular to the vertical mound, and continue rolling the pancake to the right to create an enclosed fajita roll-up. My son Julian can eat 2 big ones—how many can you have?

FILET MIGNON WITH ONIONS, MUSHROOMS & BLACK PEPPER SAUCE

蘑菇蠔油牛柳 **Serves 4**

This dish is worth every penny. Tender cubes of filet mignon and a light brown sauce with crunchy onions and thick-cut mushrooms—delicious. Something to keep in mind: The use of high heat is imperative, as you want to get a good sear on the filet. The timing here should produce a medium-rare steak, but feel free to decrease or increase the cook time to your liking.

1¼ pounds filet mignon, cut into 1¼-inch cubes

Marinade

1 tablespoon oyster sauce

1 teaspoon dark soy sauce

1 teaspoon soy sauce

1 tablespoon Shaoxing rice wine

1 teaspoon cornstarch, plus more for slurry

¼ teaspoon garlic powder

3 tablespoons vegetable oil

4 tablespoons vegetable oil

1 small yellow onion, peeled and diced into 1-inch pieces

8 ounces button mushrooms, stems removed and sliced into ½-inch thick pieces

1 teaspoon soy sauce

6 turns freshly ground black pepper

Prep list

MAKE THE MARINADE: In a medium bowl, combine the marinade ingredients, add the steak, and mix well. Marinate for at least 1 hour in the refrigerator.

MAKE A CORNSTARCH SLURRY: In a small bowl, combine 1 teaspoon of cornstarch with 2 teaspoons of water, mixing until smooth. If the cornstarch and water separate over time, you may need to mix again before using.

PREPARE AND MEASURE the remaining ingredients.

Cooking

Heat a large pan over high heat. Once the pan is hot, add 4 tablespoons of the oil. When it shimmers, add the filet mignon and stir-fry until the beef begins to brown, about 2 to 3 minutes. Increase or decrease cooking time to your preference—1 minute more will get you medium to well done. For a rare preparation, decrease your overall cooking time by 1 minute.

Add the onions, the mushrooms, the soy sauce, and the black pepper. Cook until the mushrooms are tender and the onions are slightly softened but still crunchy, about 2 minutes more.

Add the cornstarch slurry and cook until the sauce thickens, about 1 minute. Remove from the pan, plate, and serve.

GRANDMA'S BEIJING MEAT SAUCE

炸酱面 **Serves 4 to 6**

My grandmother, who I called Lau Lau or (姥姥), was born in 1927 to an aristocratic family. Growing up in Beijing, she had chefs and servants and wasn't allowed in the kitchen. Lau Lau was not a trained chef or even a cook, but as a little girl visiting her kitchen, she sure fooled me. My favorite dish of hers was zha jiang mian, a meat sauce that is similar to a Bolognese. Of all my childhood food memories, this is one of the warmest.

When my grandmother was diagnosed with cancer, I took her to chemotherapy appointments and cooked this sauce with her. I brought a scale and weighed ingredients as she spooned them out. Before she passed, I told her I was going to share her zha jiang mian with as many people as possible. It gives me such joy and a sense of peace to share this dish, not only through Dumpling Daughter, but now in this book, so that you too can share it with your loved ones.

6 tablespoons vegetable oil

4 cloves garlic, peeled and thinly sliced

1 large yellow onion, peeled and diced

1 pound ground pork, 80% lean

1 tablespoon Shaoxing rice wine

1 cup hoisin sauce

2 tablespoons Tian Mian Jiang (sweet bean paste)

12 ounces five spice tofu (or substitute with 14 ounces well-dried, extra firm tofu), diced into ¼-inch cubes

1 tablespoon XO sauce

1 pound dry white noodles

1 English cucumber

Cooking

Heat a large pan over medium heat. Once the pan is hot, add the oil. When it shimmers, add the garlic and the onion. Cook until the onion is tender, about 8 minutes.

Add the ground pork and cook continuously, crumbling it into smaller bits. (I like to use a metal soup ladle to really press down and break it apart.) Cook until the pork begins to brown, about 3 minutes.

Add the wine and cook until absorbed, about 1 minute. Add the hoisin sauce, the sweet bean paste, and ½ cup water, and mix well. Reduce heat to medium-low and simmer for 4 minutes. Add the tofu and the XO sauce, and continue to simmer until the tofu is warmed through, about 2 minutes.

Cook your noodles according to the package directions. While the noodles cook, prepare the cucumber garnish by cutting into matchsticks.

When the noodles are done and drained, portion them out in individual pasta bowls and ladle a generous amount of the sauce over the steaming noodles. Garnish with the julienned cucumbers.

This sauce will keep well in the refrigerator for up to 5 days. Freeze in small batches to enjoy for up to 6 months.

SCALLION LO MEIN

香葱拷麵 **Serves 4**

My parents weren't the only restauranteurs in the family. My mother's sister, Wilma, and her husband, Rick, were also in the restaurant business. At one point, between the two of them, the sisters owned and operated over ten restaurants. I just loved visiting my aunt and uncle's restaurants. My favorite was Weylu's Palace. Its Pagoda-like architecture cut a distinctive shape along Route 1 in Saugus. On the top floor, there was a Japanese hibachi restaurant called Midori—to me, this was where all the action happened. My favorite dish there was "garlic noodles," a simple but delicious plate of sautéed yellow noodles. I set out to recreate it at home so that I could have it anytime a craving hit. Like the teppanyaki from my childhood, this Scallion Lo Mein is heavy on the garlic. I love sharing this dish with kids, who tend to devour it as I do. Sometimes I like to stand next to the chef at Dumpling Daughter just to smell the noodles—it brings me right back to Midori.

12 ounces fresh egg noodles (or substitute with 8 ounces dry spaghetti)

1 tablespoon butter

1 tablespoon vegetable oil

4 scallions, trimmed and cut into 2-inch pieces

5 cloves garlic, peeled and thinly sliced

2 tablespoons soy sauce

1½ tablespoons sugar

Prep list

COOK THE NOODLES according to package instructions, until al dente. Blanch in ice water and strain to prevent the noodles from sticking.

PREPARE AND MEASURE the remaining ingredients.

Cooking

Heat a large pan over high heat. Add the butter and the oil. When the butter has melted and the oil is hot, add the scallions and the garlic and sauté until fragrant and the garlic is golden, about 30 seconds.

Add the cooked noodles to the pan, breaking them apart and tossing with tongs. Add the soy sauce and the sugar, tossing well to ensure the noodles are evenly coated. Cook until the noodles are warmed through, about 90 seconds.

SHRIMP WITH LOBSTER SAUCE (BOSTON STYLE)

虾龙湖 **Serves 4**

The story of American-Chinese cuisine, like others from immigrant cultures, is really a story of persistence and innovation—and this dish is no exception. Using what was readily available and would sell, entrepreneurial restauranteurs created this dish specifically for American palates, but even along the Eastern seaboard, the dish varies. New York style is differentiated from Boston style by the amount of soy sauce and the way eggs are incorporated. You'll probably notice that there is no lobster in this sauce—it's not a misnomer, but rather a nod to the dressing used on that more formidable crustacean. If you're curious about that dish, have a look at Lobster Cantonese Style (pg. 76).

1 pound shrimp (16-20 per pound)

Sauce

½ cup chicken broth

2 tablespoons soy sauce

1 tablespoon Shaoxing rice wine

1 teaspoon sugar

---

1 small yellow onion, peeled and diced

3 cloves garlic, peeled and chopped

3 tablespoons dòuchǐ (fermented black beans), soaked overnight and rinsed thoroughly

4 ounces ground pork

1 tablespoon cornstarch

½ cup vegetable oil, divided

1 egg

2 scallions, trimmed and chopped

Prep list

MAKE THE SAUCE: In a small bowl, combine the sauce ingredients and mix well.

PEEL AND DEVEIN THE SHRIMP, then rinse with cold water. Pat the shrimp dry with a paper towel.

MAKE THE PORK MIXTURE: In a medium bowl, combine the onions, the garlic, the fermented black beans, and the ground pork and mix.

MAKE A CORNSTARCH SLURRY: In a small bowl, combine 1 tablespoon of cornstarch with 1 tablespoon of water, mixing until smooth. If the cornstarch and water separate over time, you may need to mix again before using.

PREPARE AND MEASURE the remaining ingredients.

Cooking

Heat a large pan over high heat. Once the pan is hot, add ¼ cup of the oil. When it shimmers, add the shrimp and cook until pink, about 2 minutes. Remove and set aside on a serving platter.

Heat the same pan over medium heat. Add the remaining ¼ cup of oil. When it's hot, add the pork mixture and cook until the pork is opaque, about 2 minutes. Add the sauce and the shrimp, and cook until the sauce bubbles, about 2 minutes.

Crack the egg into the pan and mix until cooked and the sauce has thickened. Stir until the consistency is like gravy, coating the shrimp. If the sauce looks watery, turn the heat to high and slowly add the cornstarch slurry while mixing the shrimp and the pork. If the sauce does not appear watery, you do not need the slurry.

Add the scallions and mix well.

COCO'S ROLL-UPS

牛肉卷饼 **Serves 4**

Back in 2013, when I was writing the menu for Dumpling Daughter, my mother insisted I offer a scallion pancake roll, a traditional street food from Taiwan that falls somewhere between a burrito and a sandwich. I'd eaten them in Asia but hadn't considered adding it to the menu until my mom made some for my sister and me. Nicole and I nodded and smiled—this dish had to be on the menu. My sister's nickname was Coco, so I named the dish to mark that moment. While this is a specific recipe for a Dumpling Daughter favorite, get creative. Make scallion pancake roll-ups with scrambled eggs, pork sung, or tofu—yum!

4 Scallion Pancakes, pg. 163

24 thin slices Beef Shank, pg. 38

4 tablespoons hoisin sauce

2 scallions, trimmed and chopped

2 sprigs cilantro, chopped

On a cooked and crisp scallion pancake, neatly spread 6 thin slices of beef shank. Spread 1 tablespoon of hoisin sauce across the beef.

Sprinkle the scallions and the cilantro over the beef shank. Tightly roll up the pancake and cut in half on a diagonal to serve.

Repeat with the remaining ingredients.

Eggplant Two Ways: **MOTHER & DAUGHTER**

I am not a huge eggplant fan, but I absolutely love these two incredibly delicious recipes. The first, a classic Chinese eggplant dish, is my mom's version. It's both simple and sweet, and a real crowd-pleaser. The Dumpling Daughter version is a Yu-Hsiang style eggplant dish, with lots of garlic and spice. This is one of the most popular items on our menu for a good reason! No matter which recipe you try, serve it over rice to soak up the flavorful juices.

MOM'S EGGPLANT

媽咪茄子   **Serves 4**

¾ cup vegetable oil

1½ pounds Chinese eggplant, cut obliquely into 1-inch thick slices, 2 to 3 inches long

6 cloves garlic, peeled and thinly sliced

½ cup chicken broth

⅓ cup hoisin sauce

3 scallions, trimmed and cut into 2-inch pieces

Heat the oil in a large pan over high heat until it shimmers. The oil should be about 350°F.

Add the eggplant and the garlic and cook for about 3 minutes, tossing the eggplant in the pan to maintain its beautiful purple color.

Add the chicken broth, reduce heat to medium, and cover. Simmer until the eggplant is tender and has absorbed the chicken broth, about 7 minutes. Then add the hoisin sauce and the scallions and stir.

There may be residual oil. Using a slotted spoon, carefully remove the eggplant and the sauce, leaving any excess oil in the pan.

DUMPLING DAUGHTER EGGPLANT

鱼香茄子   **Serves 4**

¾ cup vegetable oil

1½ pounds Chinese eggplant, cut obliquely into 1-inch thick slices, about 2 to 3 inches long

6 cloves garlic, peeled and minced

½ cup chicken broth

¼ cup Sambal Olek (red chili paste)

3 scallions, trimmed and cut into 2-inch pieces

1 teaspoon salt

Heat the oil in a large pan over high heat until it shimmers. The oil should be about 350°F.

Add the eggplant and cook for about 3 minutes, tossing it in the pan to maintain its beautiful purple color.

Add the garlic, the chicken broth, and the Sambal Olek. Mix to incorporate. Reduce heat to medium and cover. Simmer until the eggplant is tender and has absorbed the chicken broth, about 7 minutes. Add the scallions and the salt and mix to incorporate.

There may be residual oil. Using a slotted spoon, carefully remove the eggplant and the sauce, leaving any excess oil in the pan.

SCALLION PANCAKES

葱油饼 **Yields seven 8-inch pancakes**

Our pastry chef, Sao Shan, made the scallion pancakes fresh at Sally Ling's from the early 1980s until we closed in 2003. I loved watching Sao Shan work with dough, constantly creating new treats both savory and sweet. She would stand at the five-foot-long stainless steel table in the center of the kitchen and roll a sheet of dough the same size. Her recipe for scallion pancakes made at least forty at a time, and the entire process was clean and efficient. This is her recipe, and it yields several pancakes because that's how she'd do it. Making fresh dough and going through the process is a commitment, so it's best to make a lot at once and freeze them for future use. Once the pancakes are formed, simply stack them on top of each other with a sheet of parchment paper or plastic wrap between them. Seal the entire stack of pancakes with plastic wrap and freeze. You don't even have to thaw them—just sear them while they're frozen.

This recipe calls for a kitchen thermometer. If you don't have one handy, don't worry—just make sure the water is warm enough that you could take a bath in it.

4 cups all-purpose flour, plus more for rolling

2½ teaspoons salt, divided

1⅓ cups warm water, approximately 100°F

4 tablespoons vegetable oil, divided, plus more for cooking

2 bunches scallions, trimmed and chopped

Mixing Dough

In a medium mixing bowl, whisk together the flour and ½ teaspoon of the salt.

Drizzle in half of the water, mixing with chopsticks to combine. The dough will be flaky before it comes together—be patient. Slowly add the rest of the water and continue mixing with your hands. If the dough is wet and sticky, add more flour, 1 tablespoon at a time. The dough should be moist but not sticking to your hands. Add 1 tablespoon of the oil and mix. Cover the bowl with a damp paper towel and let rest for 15 minutes at room temperature.

After resting, knead the dough on a floured surface for about 1 minute. The dough should be smooth and spring back when poked. Return the dough to the bowl, cover with a damp paper towel, and let it rest again for 1 hour.

While the dough is resting, trim and chop the scallions. (I like to cut the white part of the scallions in half lengthwise before chopping.) Place the scallions in a bowl, add ½ teaspoon of the salt, and toss.

Rolling and Shaping Pancakes

On a floured surface, roll and stretch the dough into a large rectangle that measures about 21 inches by 18 inches and ¼ inch thick. (When rolled out, the dough should be about the size of a full sheet pan, which will look very large.) Continue to sprinkle with flour as needed to prevent the dough from sticking to the counter surface.

Evenly sprinkle 1½ teaspoons of the salt over the entire surface of the dough. Pour 3 tablespoons of the oil in a stream down the center of the dough, then spread the oil over its entire surface. (One trick is to lightly fold the dough over itself in multiple directions so that the oil coats the dough evenly; another trick is to use a basting brush.)

Lightly sprinkle 1 teaspoon of flour over the dough to absorb any excess oil. Sprinkle the scallions evenly over the entire surface of the dough.

Working from the longest side of the rectangle, roll the dough away from you as you would a cinnamon bun to create a tight rope, then cut 3-inch lengths to portion out 7 rolls.

Tuck the scallions into the dough by pushing into the center, then crimp the outer layer of the coil together so that the scallions will stay enclosed. Do this on both sides of the dough rolls, then bring the crimped ends together and pinch, creating a ball with a knot at the top. (It will look like a steamed bun.) Delicately place on a floured surface with the knot side down. Continue until all 7 balls are portioned and shaped.

Flatten each ball with the palm of your hand. Using a rolling pin, roll out the pancakes until the diameter is about 8-inches and the pancake is no more than ¼ inch thick. Always start in the center and roll toward the edges to maintain even thickness. As you're rolling, flip the pancake and lightly dust with flour as needed to prevent it from sticking and to keep the scallions from escaping.

Cooking

Heat a large pan over medium heat. Once the pan is hot, add 2 tablespoons of the oil. When it shimmers, place the pancake in the pan. Let it cook until the surface is golden, about 3 minutes, and flip with a spatula. Be careful of splattering oil! It is a good idea to peek under the pancake often.

The cooking time for the second side will vary depending on multiple factors: temperature, the amount of oil in the pan, and the amount of excess flour on the pancake. If it becomes dry and starts to burn, add more oil, ½ tablespoon at a time and/or reduce the heat. Continue cooking and flipping as needed until both sides are golden and crispy.

Turn the pancakes onto a cutting board, dab with a paper towel to remove excess oil, and slice into wedges or use the pancake for a roll-up. If you've never tried that, see Coco's Roll-Ups (pg. 159). Otherwise serve with Perfect Dumpling Sauce (pg. 41), or Dumpling Daughter Red Chili Oil (pg. 45).

BABY BOK CHOY WITH FRESH GARLIC

 **Serves 4**

This dish of sautéed, flavorful leafy greens and fresh garlic is a great addition to any meal. Make sure to use baby bok choy here—not the regular size. Small bok choy are far more tender. Also, keep in mind that bok choy tends to have sediment between the leaves, so it is important to cut it first before washing to get it clean. Last note: this recipe uses chicken broth; if you'd like to make it vegan, simply use vegetable broth instead. I like to cook this as a side dish.

8 small baby bok choy (about 1 pound)

4 tablespoons vegetable oil

6 cloves garlic, peeled and thinly sliced

¼ cup chicken broth

1 teaspoon salt

Prep list

TRIM THE ROOT ENDS, then quarter the bok choy by cutting it in half lengthwise, and then in half lengthwise again. Soak and rinse the bok choy several times to ensure all sediment is washed away.

PREPARE AND MEASURE the remaining ingredients.

Cooking

Heat a large pan over high heat. Once the pan is hot, add the oil. When it shimmers, add the garlic and toast until golden, no more than 30 seconds.

Add the bok choy and cook until it begins to wilt, about 2 minutes, tossing frequently. Add the chicken broth and the salt. Cover and let simmer until the bok choy is soft and tender, about 1 to 2 minutes.

CRAB RANGOONS

蟹肉饺 **Yields 30 to 35 crab rangoons**

The first time I had crab rangoons was at Weylu's, my aunt and uncle's restaurant on Route 1 in Saugus. I remember sinking my teeth into my first one: crispy, smooth, creamy and oh my—life changing. These don't exist in China, as cheese is rarely used there. My parents' restaurants never offered crab rangoons, but I included them on the Dumpling Daughter menu, because (selfishly) I wanted on-demand access. Luckily, I've realized this recipe can easily be made at home using wonton skins, which are readily available in most supermarkets.

Stuffing

1 stalk celery, finely minced and squeezed in a paper towel to remove excess water

2 scallions, trimmed and chopped

2 tablespoons water chestnuts, finely minced

Shredded parmesan cheese (about 1 ounce)

8 ounces cream cheese

6 ounces crab meat, drained (claw or lump meat preferred)

⅛ teaspoon white pepper

35 wonton skins

3 cups vegetable oil, for frying

> *Prep list*
>
> IN A MEDIUM BOWL, combine the stuffing ingredients and mix with your hands until fully incorporated.
>
> LINE A BAKING SHEET with paper towels for the finished crab rangoons.
>
> PREPARE AND MEASURE the remaining ingredients.

Wrapping

Wrap the crab rangoons: Place the wonton skin at a 45-degree angle to you. Place about 1 tablespoon of filling in the center of the wonton skin. Paint water on all edges of the skin and fold it over the filling, creating a triangle. Seal by pinching tightly along all edges to prevent air from getting trapped inside. Uncooked crab rangoons can be frozen for up to 3 months. They can be fried from frozen, following the same directions as below.

Cooking

Over medium heat, bring the oil to 375°F in a medium sauce pot. (A pot about 6 to 8 inches in diameter works best; you will require less oil and limit the mess.)

Using a slotted metal spoon, gently place the crab rangoons in the oil. Fry them until golden, about 1 minute. To make sure both sides are crispy, hold the crab rangoons down with the slotted metal spoon. The crab rangoons will float when they are done. Remove with the slotted metal spoon and transfer to the prepared baking sheet to absorb the excess oil. Fry in batches of 2 to 4.

Serve with Gourmet Duck Sauce (pg. 42) and enjoy with a Mai Tai or a Scorpion Bowl!

DAN DAN MIEN

THIS (ADDICTIVE) SICHUAN STREET FOOD translates to Noodles Carried on a Pole—referring to the way street vendors would carry their pots of noodles sold to passers-by. Traditionally, the noodles are immersed in a thick red chili oil, but like all traditional dishes, every family and chef has their own version. It's supposed to be spicy and feature minced pork and preserved mustard greens, which give the dish its complex, layered flavor. You will likely need to shop online or visit your local Chinese market to find the sui mi ya cai, the preserved mustard greens, but it's the key to the dish, providing the unique fermented tang common to many classic Sichuan dishes.

Dan Dan Mien is hot, earthy, tangy—a noodle powerhouse, and because of this it is not usually served as a main, but rather as a side dish complementing a larger meal, or as a snack. At Dumpling Daughter, we serve the dish with a garnish of blanched bok choy—but anything on hand will do, including spinach.

TRADITIONAL DAN DAN MIEN

Dan Dan Mien is the best-selling noodle dish on the Dumpling Daughter menu—and for good reason. Once you've tried it, you can't *not* eat it—but our version is designed for American palates. I've included an authentic recipe that takes me back to my trip to Chongqing.

Prepare the pork topping as you would for the Dumpling Daughter's Dan Dan Mien (see next page) until the final step. (We're going to increase the chili oil to ½ cup—watch out!)

1 tablespoon sesame sauce

1 teaspoon dark soy sauce

½ cup Dumpling Daughter Red Chili Oil, pg. 45.

Handful of blanched baby bok choy or spinach leaves

Prepare your noodles according to package directions. Pour the sesame sauce and the dark soy sauce in the bottom of the serving bowl. Strain the noodles and plate over the sauce. Pour the chili oil around the perimeter of the noodles. Pile on the minced pork topping and blanched baby bok choy or spinach. Enjoy as you would in Chongqing!

DUMPLING DAUGHTER'S DAN DAN MIEN

担担面 **Serves 4 to 6**

2 tablespoons sui mi ya cai
(preserved mustard greens)

4 tablespoons vegetable oil

4 cloves garlic, peeled

8 ounces ground pork

1 tablespoon soy sauce

1 tablespoon sugar

1 teaspoon cornstarch

1 teaspoon sesame oil

8 ounces dry white noodles

¾ cup Sesame Sauce, pg. 42

3 tablespoons Dumpling
Daughter Red Chili Oil, pg. 45

Handful of blanched baby bok
choy or spinach

Prep list

SUBMERGE THE SUI MI YA CAI in ½ cup of water and set aside for at least 30 minutes. The water absorbs and removes some of the salt preservatives in the greens. Drain and squeeze the water out before cooking.

PREPARE AND MEASURE the remaining ingredients.

Cooking

Heat a large pan over medium heat. Once the pan is hot, add the vegetable oil. When it shimmers, add the whole cloves of garlic and toast until golden, about 30 seconds. Remove and discard the garlic.

Add the pork and break it into minced pieces, cooking until it is opaque, about 2 minutes. Add the soy sauce and the sugar and mix well. Add the cornstarch to absorb the liquid and fat. Add the sui mi ya cai and mix to combine. Remove from heat.

Drizzle the sesame oil and toss. Set aside until ready to plate and serve. (The pork can be refrigerated for up to 5 days.)

Prepare your noodles according to package directions. Strain the noodles and plate in a large shallow bowl. Drizzle with the sesame sauce and top with the pork mixture. Finish by drizzling the chili oil on the perimeter of the sauce and pork so that you can see the red oil on the white noodles. Add blanched baby bok choy or spinach on top. Serve immediately or the noodles will stick together!

SESAME WONTONS

芝麻云吞 **Serves 4**

Remember when I suggested you make extra dumplings and wontons and stash them in your freezer? Well, here's why. This is one of the easiest and most satisfying uses of pre-made wontons, sesame sauce, and chili oil. When I cooked this for Guy Fieri on the Food Network show Guy's Grocery Games, he said, "How about you just win the whole show with this dish?!"

24 Homemade Wontons, pg. 82

½ cup Sesame Sauce, pg. 42

½ cup Dumpling Daughter Red Chili Oil, pg. 45

2 scallions, greens only, trimmed and chopped

½ cup cilantro leaves, removed from stems, washed, and dried

Cooking and Assembling

Bring 6 cups of water to a boil over high heat. Carefully place the wontons into the boiling water. Immediately stir with a slotted spoon to prevent them from sticking to the bottom and sides. Boil the wontons over high heat for about 3 minutes, gently stirring occasionally. (Frozen wontons may take a minute longer.) Once the wontons float, cook for another minute or so. Take one out to test it! The internal temperature should be 165°F, and the filling should be cooked through.

Remove the wontons with a slotted spoon and plate on a large platter. Drizzle with the sesame sauce and the chili oil, and garnish with the scallions and the cilantro leaves—savor each delicate work of art!

WOK ROASTED STRING BEANS WITH PRESERVED MUSTARD GREENS

干扁四季豆　**Serves 2 to 4**

These string beans are so good, we call them green French fries. (Julian eats them the same way, too!) It's a quick and easy dish, perfect for a weeknight meal. You won't use an entire package of preserved mustard greens to make this dish, but they save in the refrigerator for weeks. I have a friend who tosses them in her scrambled eggs!

3 tablespoons sui mi ya cai
　(preserved mustard greens)

½ cup vegetable oil

1 large clove garlic, peeled
　and minced

½-inch piece fresh ginger root,
　peeled and minced

1 pound string beans, trimmed

1 scallion, trimmed and chopped

½ teaspoon sugar

1 teaspoon salt

1 teaspoon Peppercorn Oil,
　pg. 46

Prep list

SUBMERGE THE SUI MI YA CAI in ½ cup of water and set aside for at least 30 minutes. The water absorbs and removes some of the salt preservatives in the greens. Drain and squeeze the water out before cooking.

PREPARE AND MEASURE the remaining ingredients.

Cooking

Heat a large pan over medium heat. Once the pan is hot, add the vegetable oil. When it shimmers, add the garlic, the ginger, and the string beans, and cook until the beans are tender, about 8 minutes.

Add ¼ cup of water and the mustard greens, cover and cook for about 5 minutes. Remove the lid, turn heat to high, and cook off any remaining water. Remove from heat, add the scallions, the sugar, the salt, and the Peppercorn Oil. Mix well.

Remove the string beans with a slotted spoon or tongs, making sure to leave residual oil behind. Plate and serve as a side.

SHREDDED PORK WITH PICKLED MUSTARD NOODLE SOUP

榨菜肉丝面 **Serves 1**

I enjoy this delicious noodle soup at breakfast and lunch. Use the Sparerib Daikon Soup (pg. 81) or From Scratch Chicken Broth (pg. 39) as the base, but any light bone broth in your freezer also works. The shredded pork is tender and light and the zhàcài (pickled mustard) provides a burst of earthy flavor.

4 ounces lean pork loin, shredded into thin 2-inch strips

Marinade

1 teaspoon salt

½ teaspoon white pepper

1 teaspoon cornstarch

1 teaspoon water

1 teaspoon vegetable oil

⅓ cup zhàcài (Sichuan pickled mustard)

2 cups chicken broth

3 ounces dry white noodles

1 scallion, trimmed and chopped into 1-inch long pieces

½ teaspoon sesame oil

Prep list

MAKE THE MARINADE: Place the pork in a medium bowl. One by one, add the marinade ingredients in the order listed above, and massage them into the pork.

SOAK THE PICKLED MUSTARD in 1 cup of cold water for at least 5 minutes. Drain afterward.

PREPARE AND MEASURE the remaining ingredients.

Cooking

Bring the chicken broth to a boil over high heat in a 4-quart pot. Once boiling, reduce the heat to medium-low and add the pork. Separate all the pieces of pork with chopsticks or tongs to ensure they cook thoroughly. Boil until the pork is cooked through, about 3 minutes. Remove the pork from the broth with a slotted spoon, then set aside. Preserve the broth.

Meanwhile, in another pot, prepare your noodles according to package directions. Strain the noodles and place them in a noodle soup bowl.

Top the noodles with the pickled mustard, the pork, and the scallions. Pour the broth over the noodles and garnishes. Drizzle with the sesame oil and serve with a Chinese soup spoon.

EGG FLOWER TOMATO SOUP

蕃茄蛋花汤 **Serves 2**

This soup is simple but elegant and can be modified in endless ways. To pack in more flavor, add freshly chopped herbs, like scallions and cilantro. Feeling extra hungry? Add some noodles!

2 tablespoons vegetable oil

1 cup plum tomatoes, seeds removed and diced into 1-inch pieces

4 cups chicken broth

1 large egg, whisked in a small bowl

1 teaspoon salt, plus more to taste

½ teaspoon sesame oil

1 scallion, greens only, trimmed and chopped

Cooking

Heat a medium pot over low heat. Once the pan is warm, add the vegetable oil. Add the tomatoes and cook until tender, about 2 minutes. Increase heat to high, add the chicken broth, and bring to a boil.

Whisk the eggs into the soup. Add the salt to taste.

Transfer to serving bowls, and garnish with the sesame oil and the scallions.

BEEF BEIJING NOODLE SOUP

牛肉汤麪 **Serves 2**

This is my idea of the ultimate comfort noodle soup. I fell in love with it at my mother's first restaurant, Peking Cuisine in Chinatown. The broth is rich, and the Chinese white noodles are topped with delicious fresh herbs and slow-cooked beef shank. Each component involves several steps, but I promise—it's worth it. When I was six years old, waiters were impressed that I could take down a whole bowl to the last drop.

Beef Broth

2 tablespoons vegetable oil

2 scallions, trimmed and cut into 1-inch long pieces

2 tablespoons chili sauce (Sriracha or another spicy chili sauce)

4 cups reserved braising liquid from Classic Braised Beef Shank, pg. 38

---

2 tablespoons zhàcài (Sichuan pickled mustard)

8 ounces cooked white noodles

12 thin slices Classic Braised Beef Shank, pg. 38

8 branches cilantro leaves, removed from stems, washed, and dried

1 scallion, trimmed and chopped

1 teaspoon sesame oil

Prep list

SOAK THE PICKLED MUSTARD in 2 cups of cold water for at least 5 minutes. Drain afterward.

PREPARE AND MEASURE the remaining ingredients.

Cooking

Make the beef broth: Add the vegetable oil to a 6-quart pot over medium heat. When it's hot, add the scallions and the chili sauce, and sauté for about 1 to 2 minutes, or until the scallions are wilted and their aroma is released. Add the braising liquid and heat until almost boiling. Stir and strain out the scallions and chili sauce.

Cook the noodles according to package directions. Strain and divide them among 2 serving bowls.

If necessary, reheat the beef broth. Build each bowl by garnishing the noodles with 6 slices of the beef shank in a fan-like formation, 1 tablespoon of pickled mustard, half the chopped cilantro, and half the chopped scallion. Drizzle ½ teaspoon of sesame oil over the top.

Ladle the warmed beef broth over the noodles, carefully pouring over all the beef and garnishes to warm them up. Serve hot!

CHOOSE YOUR OWN DUMPLING DAUGHTER ADVENTURE

Operating three restaurants keeps me busy. When I stop by a Dumpling Daughter, I'm usually famished. So I grab a bowl and get creative. What I choose to eat each day relies completely on my mood, and I rarely eat the same thing two days in a row. Many of the dishes and specials on our menu came from a place of hunger and putting prepared ingredients together on the fly. If I want something light, I go heavy on the vegetables. When I crave a hearty dish, I usually pick beef broth or rice with beef shank, lots of sauces, and fresh herbs like scallions and cilantro. This section aims to provide a mix-and-match foundation for creating your own dishes, plus a few of our favorite combinations. It is especially great when you have a fridge full of leftovers. Have fun with it!

BASES

Rice (plain or fried), pgs. 128, 148, 221

Noodles

Taiwanese bun

PROTEINS

Soy-Braised Pork Belly, pg. 214

Home Fried Chicken, pg. 134

Pan-seared or steamed tofu

Pan-seared, steamed, or fried fish

Beef Shank, pg. 38

Fried egg or Mom's Marbled Tea Egg, pg. 48

Ma-Po Sauce, pg. 124

Grandma's Meat Sauce, pg. 154

Dan Dan Mien (topping only), pg. 172

Handmade Wontons, pg. 82

BROTHS (for noodle soups)

Vegetable Broth, pg. 40

Chicken Broth, pg. 39

Beef Broth, pg. 38

VEGETABLES

Carrot, cut into matchsticks

Cucumber, cut into matchsticks

Pickled radish, cut into matchsticks

Purple cabbage, shredded

Kimchi

Tomato, finely diced

Mustard greens, shredded

GARNISHES

Scallion

Cilantro

Nori seaweed

Sesame seeds

SAUCES

Dumpling Daughter Red Chili Oil, pg. 45

Dumpling Daughter Spicy Sweet Soy

Sriracha or another spicy chili sauce

Kewpie

Mike's Hot Honey

Dumpling Daughter Sweet Soy

Peppercorn Oil, pg. 46

Sesame Sauce, pg. 42

Rice Bowls

COOK THE RICE (white or brown) according to package instructions. Place about one cup of cooked rice in a serving bowl. Drizzle the desired sauces over the top. Place the protein over the rice and the vegetables neatly next to the protein. Top with the garnishes. Drizzle more sauce over the bowl.

SALMON RICE BOWL

Rice	Kewpie
Steamed salmon	Cucumber, cut into matchsticks
Dumpling Daughter Spicy Sweet Soy	Scallions, chopped
Sriracha or another spicy chili sauce	Nori seaweed

PORK BELLY RICE BOWL

Rice	Mom's Marbled Tea Egg, cut in half, pg. 48
Soy-Braised Pork Belly (including braising liquid), pg. 214	Scallions, chopped
Pickled Radish, shredded	Dumpling Daughter Red Chili Oil, pg. 45

Noodles

COOK THE NOODLES according to package instructions. Place about one cup of cooked noodles in a serving bowl. Drizzle the desired sauces over top. Place the protein over the noodles and the vegetables neatly next to the protein. Top with the garnishes. Drizzle more sauce over the bowl. If making noodle soup, pour enough broth into the bowl to cover the ingredients, heating up the garnishes to release their flavors.

THE WORKS

White noodles	Sesame Sauce, pg. 42
Dumpling Daughter Red Chili Oil, pg. 45	Grandma's Meat Sauce, pg. 154
Peppercorn Oil, pg. 46	Cilantro, chopped

LIGHT NOODLE SOUP

White Noodles	Cilantro, chopped
Beef shank, sliced, pg. 38	Cucumber, cut into matchsticks
Chicken Broth, pg. 39	Kimchi
Tomato, diced	Scallions

Taiwanese Buns

STEAM 2 TO 3 TAIWANESE BUNS according to package instructions. Carefully pull the 2 halves of the buns apart, trying not to rip the bread, and rest them open-faced on a cutting board. Place the protein on the base of the bun first, then top with the vegetables and the sauce. Carefully fold the two halves back together like a clam shell and use a skewer to hold everything in place.

PORK BELLY TAIWANESE BUNS

Taiwanese Buns

Soy-Braised Pork Belly, pg. 214

Cucumber, cut into matchsticks

Hoisin sauce

Cilantro leaves

VEGETABLE TAIWANESE BUNS

Taiwanese Buns

Carrots, cut into matchsticks

Cucumbers, cut into matchsticks

Pickled Radish, cut into matchsticks

Sriracha

Kewpie

Scallions, chopped

Cilantro, chopped

FEEDING MY FAMILY

Homestyle Cooking and Cozy Entertaining

Cucumber Salad Two Ways:

Sally Ling's Cucumber Salad

Nadia's Cucumber Salad

Jumbo Shrimp with Snow Peas

Chicken with Broccoli

Butter Miso Noodles

Cod with Tomato, Capers & Ginger

Steamed Halibut with Ginger & Scallions

Rice Noodles Singapore Style

Bean Sprouts with Sichuan Peppercorn

Shrimp Lo Mein with Spaghetti

Spicy Beef with Hot Italian Peppers

**Yu-Hsiang Shredded Pork with
Wood Ear Mushrooms**

Pork Chop Homestyle

Soy-Braised Pork Belly

Sautéed Fish Balls

Ma-La Noodle Salad

Fried Rice with Dates, Pineapple & Scallions

**Braised Soy Sauce Whole Fish
with Organic Tofu**

Shredded Beef with Cilantro

Chicken with Celery & Carrots

I ALWAYS KNEW I WANTED CHILDREN, AND THAT BECOMING A MOTHER WOULD COMPLETE MY LIFE. But before I started a family, I had to fulfill my own needs and passions. I knew that once I had a child, they would become my number one priority, so I purposely put off children until I felt self-sufficient. I had to establish my business first so that I could dedicate my whole self to the process. At the same time, I started to feel anxious, because opening Dumpling Daughter took such a long time. After the restaurant had been open for a year, I felt like I was ready. I had a manager and a head chef that I trusted. I worked every day from open to close, but I felt like I could become pregnant and still be there as much as possible. Most importantly, I always wanted to have a child with the same zodiac sign as my dad and my mom. My dad was born in the Year of the Monkey, and I really wanted a monkey of my own. I cut it close, but in December of 2016, I became a mother to Julian, my first son and my very own monkey! A few years later, we welcomed a second baby boy, Dillan, during the Year of the Rat, just like my mom.

As someone who lives and breathes food, you may not be surprised that food played a huge role in both my pregnancy and the early days of motherhood. I thoroughly enjoyed being pregnant and put a lot of thought into eating the right foods to grow my baby. I treated myself incredibly well during my pregnancies, eating a varied diet of the healthiest foods. Learning that the baby's brain grows the most in the last three months, I ate an entire mackerel at least three times a week. I was blessed with healthy babies.

In the Chinese culture, after giving birth, a new mother must stay home for thirty days without leaving the house. The idea is to take total care of the mother, so that she can take care of the baby. These early days should include a diet made up of soothing chicken soup, fish soup from live whole fish, pigs feet stew, and many other natural foods meant to strengthen the body and help produce milk. When I gave birth, my mom came to live with me, cooking for me and caring for me so I could nurse my son and sleep when I needed. Many postpartum moms struggle in the early days, but I enjoyed this time immensely. I felt so loved and comforted.

As a mom, I first and foremost want to take good care of my kids and make sure they have the necessities to live. For me, this starts with food—and I take feeding my kids very seriously. From their first bites, I paid attention, believing that if I served them healthy vegetables and proteins, they'd be great eaters for life and love their first foods forever. I started them on kale, spinach, peas, and beans, eventually introducing fish. The next item was naturally dumplings! I took great care to make my babies dumplings, using pork from our local farm, then gently breaking them apart and feeding them so they could grasp it with their tiny fingers. I still have so much fun watching them experience new foods, new textures, flavors, and temperatures. I love watching their facial reactions when they eat, knowing they are experiencing something new.

Next, I want to inspire my kids, just as my parents have inspired me. From a young age, I want them to see that both their mom and dad work hard. I want them to see that if you follow your passion and do something you love, you will feel successful. I want them to know that during their young lives, I opened up more restaurants. I started selling our dumplings online and at markets around Boston. And that our business not only survived, but thrived, even during a global pandemic.

Let me back up for a minute. After years of looking for a Cambridge location, only to pivot and open in Weston, that old urge to open in Cambridge returned—but now I had my sights set on the Kendall Square neighborhood. Kendall Square is a hub of technology and science, featuring a diverse demographic of young

I want them to see that if you follow your passion and do something you love, you will feel successful.

people, MIT students, and plenty of out-of-towners there for college visits and meetings. There is a strong international presence in the neighborhood, and I knew I could offer something different than a salad, sandwich, or pizza. My dad had always encouraged me to "bridge the gap" between easterners and westerners, and what better place to do this than in Kendall Square? I wanted Dumpling Daughter Cambridge to be a meeting place for all.

I had my eye on a distinctive location. I asked my broker to reach out to the landlord as soon as it was available. The landlord told me I could have it, under the condition that I also serve breakfast and coffee. At that time, I had no interest in expanding my concept, so I asked my sister Nicole if she wanted to create and execute her own vision. She agreed, and came up with Vester, a contemporary Swedish café. Vester reflects her own love of travel, taking inspiration from Scandinavian countries and their distinct coffee culture.

Launching the Kendall Square location was a challenge. By the time the lunch hour rolled around, the line was out the door. We had to get people through the line and served as fast as possible to maximize business at the peak lunch hour. In Weston, people don't mind waiting. In Cambridge, the expectation was that it should be as fast as possible. We had to completely change the way we did things on the backend and reinvent our operations to serve the rush and move that line. The pressure was immense. I am so glad I did not open my first restaurant in Cambridge, because it probably would have failed!

With our success in Cambridge, it was time to look for another location. Brookline was our first choice, as it is heavily residential but also has a city feel. When my father-in-law asked us to open a Dumpling Daughter in his commercial building in Coolidge Corner, we said yes immediately. Our plan was to open our Brookline location in March of 2020. Then, the unthinkable happened: a global pandemic turned the world upside-down. A week away from opening, the state mandated that restaurants be takeout only. We stalled opening to see how takeout only worked in Weston. There, we locked the door and turned to online ordering, something we'd never done before. We streamlined our menus and systems to make this new way of doing things work. A few weeks into the

pandemic, Brookline residents messaged us on social media, asking when we would open. They really wanted our food! With their excitement for our launch, we decided to open in May of 2020 with takeout only, emulating our success in Weston. We made the nightly news because we were opening a restaurant when others were closing them. We are thrilled with how well-received we've been in Brookline.

Once online ordering and contactless takeout was steady and healthy, I wanted to find new ways to excite my staff and keep them busy during these tough and uncertain times. I expressed that I wanted to do a cooking class to connect with my customers, and my young staff suggested we do virtual classes via Zoom. We thought it would be more approachable if we pre-measured and provided all the ingredients in meal kits. So soon we were busy building meal kits that the cooking class students would pick up from the restaurant. We loved connecting with our customers in this intimate and creative way. (And in many ways, it was those classes that encouraged us to write this cookbook! Our customers' curiosity about making great Chinese food at home made us want to share more and more.)

Another project that kept us very busy during the pandemic? Frozen dumplings. Yes, I was finally ready to start marketing our dumplings to the world, the original vision for Dumpling Daughter. I was in the middle of designing the box when the pandemic hit and people stopped going to the grocery stores. We decided to sell our frozen foods through our restaurants and our website, shipping our products nationwide in coolers with dry ice. People could click a few buttons and dumplings would land on their doorstep two days later, providing convenience and safety for our customers. Our dumplings were approachable and accessible, making them a new staple in kitchens nationwide.

On our way to the hospital on November 17, 2020, about to give birth to Dillan, a local family-owned farm market emailed us—they were interested in selling our dumplings and buns. I was thrilled to hear the news: if I could pick any market to carry our items, it would be Volante Farms in Needham. Other markets followed, and soon we were selling our products around the region. The Dumpling Daughter vision and dreams are coming true!

Cucumber Salad Two Ways: MOTHER & DAUGHTER

Like an amuse-bouche in French cuisine or Italian antipasto, every proper Chinese banquet starts with cold appetizers. The best part about this course? Everything is prepared in advance and chilled, so guests can enjoy it immediately upon arrival.

Every chef has their own version of this dish—my mom's recipe, a staple at Sally Ling's, is perfectly balanced: fresh, sweet, and tart with a great crunch. It is so beloved that this is the version we serve at Dumpling Daughter. When I make cucumber salad, I like to make it a bit more modern with tons of flavor. I wouldn't be able to make mine without the classic recipe, and I love building upon what I've learned from my mom.

SALLY LING'S CUCUMBER SALAD

黄瓜沙拉   **Serves 4**

2 to 3 English cucumbers (about 2 pounds), cut into batons about 3 inches long and ½ inch thick

1 tablespoon salt

Marinade

½ cup sugar

½ cup white vinegar

1 tablespoon sesame oil

1 tablespoon Peppercorn Oil, pg. 46

Prep list

IN A MEDIUM BOWL, toss the cucumbers with the salt. Cover and let sit in the refrigerator for 1 hour. Afterward, rinse the cucumbers in a strainer under cold water.

MAKE THE MARINADE: In a medium bowl, whisk the sugar and the vinegar until the sugar is fully dissolved, then add the cucumbers. For best results, cover and let sit in the refrigerator for at least 12 hours or up to 24 hours.

Strain the cucumbers and discard the marinating liquid. Toss the cucumbers with the sesame oil and the Peppercorn Oil and chill until ready to serve.

NADIA'S CUCUMBER SALAD

黄瓜沙拉   **Serves 4**

Sauce

2 cloves garlic, peeled and minced

1 tablespoon sesame oil

1 tablespoon chili oil

1 tablespoon soy sauce

Follow the instructions for Sally Ling's Cucumber Salad through the pickling step. Instead of dressing with the sesame and Peppercorn oil, try tossing it with these ingredients instead.

For more spice, add a drizzle of Peppercorn Oil (pg. 46)—or more chili oil.

JUMBO SHRIMP WITH SNOW PEAS

雪豆大虾 **Serves 4**

You can't go wrong with this beautiful, healthy dish. It is a great addition to any larger spread, as it provides a bit of lightness and crunch.

1 pound jumbo shrimp (under 12 per pound)

Sauce

2 tablespoons Shaoxing rice wine

1 teaspoon sugar

½ teaspoon salt, plus more to taste

1 teaspoon cornstarch

3 tablespoons vegetable oil

3 garlic cloves, thinly sliced

5 ounces fresh snow peas, their ends snapped to trim the strings

Prep list

PEEL AND DEVEIN THE SHRIMP, then rinse with cold water. Pat the shrimp dry with a paper towel.

MAKE THE SAUCE: In a small bowl, combine the sauce ingredients and mix well.

MAKE A CORNSTARCH SLURRY: In a small bowl, combine 1 teaspoon of cornstarch with 2 teaspoons of water, mixing until smooth. If the cornstarch and water separate over time, you may need to mix again before using.

PREPARE AND MEASURE the remaining ingredients.

Cooking

Heat a large pan over medium heat. Once the pan is hot, add the oil. When it shimmers, add the garlic and toast until golden, about 30 seconds. Remove and discard the garlic.

Add the shrimp and cook until pink, about 45 seconds.

Add the snow peas and the sauce and cook for about 2 minutes, making sure that the snow peas stay crispy.

Add the cornstarch slurry and cook until the sauce thickens, about 1 minute. Serve alongside fried rice or a richer dish.

CHICKEN WITH BROCCOLI

芥兰鸡片 **Serves 4**

Chicken with Broccoli was one of the most popular dishes at Sally Ling's—a tradition that continues today at Dumpling Daughter. At home, my husband requests it at least once a week. This is a true crowd pleaser; one you'll want to cook over and over again.

1 pound boneless, skinless chicken breast, sliced into 2- by 1- by ⅛-inch pieces

Marinade

2 teaspoons salt

3 tablespoons vegetable oil

1 teaspoon cornstarch, plus more for slurry

2 heads broccoli (about 1 pound), roughly chopped into 1-inch florets (stem peeled, if using)

½ teaspoon salt

3 tablespoons vegetable oil

4 cloves garlic, peeled

¾ cup chicken broth

Prep list

MAKE THE MARINADE: In a medium bowl, combine the marinade ingredients and the chicken and mix. Marinate for at least 30 minutes in the refrigerator.

MAKE A CORNSTARCH SLURRY: In a small bowl, combine 2 teaspoons of cornstarch with 2 tablespoons of water, mixing until smooth. If the cornstarch and water separate over time, you may need to mix again before using.

PREPARE AND MEASURE the remaining ingredients.

Cooking

Over high heat, bring 6 cups of water to a boil. Add the broccoli and blanch for 1 minute. Remove the broccoli with a slotted spoon and sprinkle with ½ teaspoon of the salt.

Heat a large pan over medium heat. Once the pan is hot, add 3 tablespoons of the oil. When it shimmers, add the garlic and toast until golden, about 30 seconds. Remove and discard the garlic.

Add the chicken, continuously stirring it, and cook until just turned white, about 2 minutes. Add the broccoli and the chicken broth, and cook until the chicken broth reduces slightly, about 1 minute, stirring occasionally. Add the cornstarch slurry and cook until the sauce thickens.

Plate and serve alongside white rice.

BUTTER MISO NOODLES

牛油黃醬麵 **Serves 2**

When we launched Dumpling Daughter, I wanted to create a kid-friendly dish that was as simple as buttered noodles, but slightly elevated. The result is like an Asian version of pasta carbonara. In a carbonara, eggs are the emulsifier; here, the noodles are tossed with a caramelized miso and butter, coating the pasta in a creamy sauce. This dish can be served as a main or a side, and goes well with almost any protein-forward dish. At Dumpling Daughter, we use spaghetti, but any pasta shape will work (Julian likes rotelle). It's sweet and savory, and is the ultimate comfort food for the 21st-century kid—or for the kids in all of us.

8 ounces dry pasta (spaghetti, fettuccini, or linguine works)

2 tablespoons white miso paste

3 tablespoons butter, cut into 3 equal parts

Prep list

COOK THE PASTA ACCORDING TO PACKAGE INSTRUCTIONS. I cook my pasta for 1 minute less than specified, as I prefer it al dente. Keep in mind, you'll be tossing it later in a hot pan, so do not overcook it.

IN A MEDIUM BOWL, mix the miso paste and 4 tablespoons of water and mix with a fork until well combined and smooth.

Cooking

Heat a medium pan over high heat. Add the butter. When the butter has melted, add the cooked pasta and the miso mixture. Gently toss the pasta with tongs and mix well. If you're feeling confident, toss it in the air—not kidding! Aerating the pasta and sauce will make it nice and creamy and ensure it's well mixed. When the pasta is warm and fully coated with the miso sauce, it's ready to serve. Have napkins on hand for the little ones!

COD WITH TOMATO, CAPERS & GINGER

甘燒酸豆鱈鱼　**Serves 2 to 4**

My mother developed this recipe while living in Florida, where she loves to entertain. It has a sweet and almost fusion feeling that her dinner guests love. I think of this dish as "nouveau" Chinese cuisine—a French preparation with a Chinese sauce. My pescatarian friends love it.

1 pound cod

¼ teaspoon white pepper, plus more to taste

1 teaspoon sea salt, plus more to taste

¼ cup all-purpose flour

Sauce

1-inch piece fresh ginger root, peeled and finely chopped

Juice of ½ lemon

3 tablespoons chicken broth

2 tablespoons ketchup

1 tablespoon Shaoxing rice wine

1 tablespoon capers

2 teaspoons sugar

⅓ cup plus 2 tablespoons vegetable oil, divided

1 plum tomato, cut into ½-inch cubes

Prep list

SPRINKLE THE WHITE PEPPER and the sea salt on both sides of the cod. Dredge in the flour and shake to remove any excess flour.

MAKE THE SAUCE: In a small bowl, combine the ginger with the lemon juice. Add the remaining sauce ingredients and mix until combined.

PREPARE AND MEASURE the remaining ingredients.

Cooking

Heat a large pan over medium-high heat. Once the pan is hot, add ⅓ cup of the oil. When it shimmers, carefully place the cod in the oil and pan-sear until golden brown on both sides, about 2 minutes each side. Remove and set aside on a serving platter.

Reduce heat to medium-low and add the remaining 2 tablespoons of oil. When it's hot, add the tomatoes and sauté until they are tender, about 3 minutes.

Add the sauce, then return the cod to the pan. Simmer for about 5 minutes. Season with the salt and the white pepper to taste.

Carefully remove the cod from the pan. Place the cod on the serving platter, being careful not to break it, then pour the sauce over the fish. A simple bowl of white rice is a great accompaniment here.

STEAMED HALIBUT WITH GINGER & SCALLIONS

薑葱蒸比目魚　*Serves 4*

This is one of my favorite dishes. It relies upon a traditional Cantonese technique that I am so excited to share. Steamed fish, fresh ginger, and scallions are topped with sizzling hot oil that flash-fries the garnishes, releasing a brilliant wave of aromatics through the kitchen. A traditional dish would call for a whole fish, but we use filets to make it more approachable. I always make extra, so I can add my leftovers to fresh salad greens the next day.

A few tips about fish: Steaming is the best way to produce tender and flaky fish. This dish works well with multiple varieties of fish, such as sea bass, haddock, cod, salmon, sole—though cooking times will vary. Try this trick from Eric Ripert: "Insert a metal skewer to the thickest part of the filet, when you remove it, touch it to the inside of your wrist (or lower lip if you're brave) and it should feel warm. If it's cold, the fish is not cooked yet; if it's hot, it is overcooked."

If you do not have a steaming basket, here's another handy trick: make balls of aluminum foil (about the size of a golf ball) and place them in the bottom of the pot. Place a baking dish on top of the aluminum foil balls, ensuring the water does not touch the baking dish. Cover and voila! You have a steaming basket.

1½ pounds halibut, skin on and no more than an inch at its thickest part

4 tablespoons light soy sauce

2 tablespoons Shaoxing rice wine

4 scallions, trimmed and julienned into 2-inch lengths

3-inch piece fresh ginger root, peeled and julienned

6 tablespoons vegetable oil, plus more for brushing

White pepper, to taste

12 sprigs cilantro, roughly chopped

Prep list

CLEAN THE FISH and pat dry with a paper towel.

IN A SMALL BOWL, combine the soy sauce and the Shaoxing rice wine. Add the scallions, ensuring they are submerged, and half the ginger.

LIGHTLY OIL A HEAT-RESISTANT PLATE and place the fish skin-side down. Sprinkle the fish with the white pepper and the rest of the ginger.

Cooking

Prepare your steamer pot and bring 2 inches of water to a boil.

Carefully place the plate of fish in the steamer and cover. Steam the fish for 8 to 10 minutes, depending on how thick your filet is. Check for doneness by inserting a metal skewer or wooden chopstick at the thickest part; if the fish is punctured without resistance, it's done. (See the headnote for tips.)

Turn off the heat, carefully remove the plate, and drain any liquid. Spread the scallion and ginger mixture across the surface of the fish, then sprinkle the chopped cilantro over top.

Here's the fun part. Heat a small pan over medium-high heat. When the pan is almost smoking, add 6 tablespoons of the oil and heat until very hot. Pour the oil over the fish and stand back—you should hear it sizzle. Serve hot, right from the sizzling plate.

RICE NOODLES SINGAPORE STYLE

星卅炒米炒 **Serves 4**

This dish never lets me down. It's rich, aromatic, and satisfying—which explains its popularity but not its origin. The use of curry is likely the result of British trade routes and inventive chefs in Hong Kong. However it came to be, these noodles have achieved worldwide fame. It is satisfying enough to be a meal in itself.

8 ounces rice noodles (I like vermicelli)

½ pound shrimp (21-25 per pound)

7 tablespoons vegetable oil, divided

2 large eggs, whisked in a small bowl

½ pound boneless, skinless chicken breast, shredded into 2-inch pieces

1 tablespoon Shaoxing rice wine

1 tablespoon oyster sauce

1 medium yellow onion, peeled and thinly sliced

1 tablespoon curry powder

2 scallions, trimmed and cut into 2-inch lengths

1 teaspoon salt

Prep list

SOAK THE RICE NOODLES in room temperature water for 30 minutes.

PEEL AND DEVEIN THE SHRIMP, then rinse with cold water. Pat the shrimp dry with a paper towel.

PREPARE AND MEASURE the remaining ingredients.

Cooking

Heat a large pan over high heat. Once the pan is hot, add 2 tablespoons of the oil. When it shimmers, add the eggs and scramble quickly, breaking the eggs up into bits until cooked through, no more than 1 minute. Remove the eggs from the pan and set aside on the platter you plan to use.

Heat the same pan over high heat. Add 2 tablespoons of the oil. When it's hot, add the chicken and the shrimp and stir-fry for about 1 minute. Cook until the chicken is opaque and the shrimp has just turned pink, then add the wine and the oyster sauce and cook, about 1 minute more. Remove and set aside with the scrambled eggs.

Heat the same pan over medium heat. Add the remaining 3 tablespoons of oil. Add the onions and cook until softened but still maintaining a bit of crunch, about 2 to 3 minutes.

Add the rice noodles, then sprinkle the curry powder over top, making sure to toss and mix well with tongs. Add ½ cup of water and the scallions and continue to stir until the noodles have absorbed the water, about 2 minutes.

Turn off the heat and return the egg, the chicken, and the shrimp to the pan. Add the salt to taste. Toss again, until evenly incorporated, then plate and serve!